Anne Nightingale
CHASE THE FADE
Music Memories
& Memorabilia

Anne Nightingale
CHASE THE FADE
Music Memories & Memorabilia

BLANDFORD PRESS
POOLE   DORSET

First published in the UK 1981 by
Blandford Press.
Link House, West Street,
Poole, Dorset BH15 1LL.

Copyright ⓒ 1981 Anne Nightingale

ISBN 0 7137 1167 1

Made by Lennard Books
The Old School
Wheathampstead
Herts AL4 8AN

Editor Michael Leitch
Art Director David Pocknell
Designer Michael Cavers
Production Reynolds Clark Associates Ltd

Printed and bound in Spain by
Novograph, S. A. Madrid
Depósito Legal: M-41.769-1980

Contents

Side A

Contents

2 x 30 min. C60

Side A *Introduction*

Ferro
Low
Noise

2 x 30 min. C60

They said: Would you like to write a book about the Seventies?

I said: No.

They said: Why not?

I said: Because if I write a book I want to sell the film rights for millions of dollars, and anyway there's all that research, and I'd leave things out like Amon Duul II and there will be far too many books about the Seventies and I don't want to write a coffee-table book and most of all I DON'T LIKE WRITING.

They said: OK, fine. We'd just like to show you some of the other books we've done.

I said: Fine. Show me. (IMPRESSED PAUSE.) Look. Well, hey, maybe there's a way around this. But I'm not putting pen to paper. Can we do it all on tape?

They said: Sure.

I said, after several months of talking in broken, half-finished sentences and using very weak adjectives the way you do in conversation: It doesn't work. I'll have to put pen to paper after all.

They said (smiling smugly): Exactly.

I said: But! I stick to my guns. No book about the Seventies.

They said: OK, how about bits of the Seventies?

I said: Well, orl-right. But it might be bits of the Sixties or bits of anything.

They said: Go on then, do it.

So I did. It's not chronological. No Extensive Research went into this. It is not a history book which you can write to *The Guardian* about complaining that the significance of Genesis is never mentioned. Remember, essentially this was written under duress, and mainly on British Rail. I'll write a real autobiography when everyone I know is dead because I'm a coward. Unless I can sell the film rights for millions of dollars, of course.

This may give you the impression that I'm a money-grabbing—or gabbing—woman who can't wait to be represented by that LA lawyer Marvin Thing. The truth is . . . it's the gas bill. And the other truth is that ten years or more ago a bloke who likes changing his name (we've been through Randy Grope, Mim, The Memphis Blueswailer, Camp, Mimsy, Ant, Tone, and, at the time of going to press, Binky—but I can't be responsible if

this is now out of date) dragged me out to see the bands I'd always wanted to see. He has pretty near total recall which is not particularly amazing except that he is quite partial to drinking a bottle of vodka of an evening. He's remembered most of the incidents mentioned in this book.

Contrary to the norm, he is *not* prepared to be The Man In The Background. He goes around shouting: 'Me, Me, Me. Recognition! Sign your autograph book, lady! I'm a star, I'm a star, I'm a starrgh . . .'

So spare a thought. Or a quid. I give you Binky. And if you think I'm alone in my affection, may I point out that five young ladies in Yorkshire, of their own volition, have founded BOOBS, the British Organization of Binky Supporters.

Anyway it's as much his book as mine. I have to say that, as he's demanding half the royalties. Goodnight.

Anne Nightingale

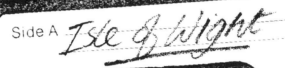

Side A Isle of Wight

Ferro
Low
Noise

2 x 30 min. C60

August 1970 among the weekend hippies at Afton Down.

The Isle of Wight in August 1970 was one of the biggest festivals ever. Not just for the staggering amount of people who came – half a million give or take a few. It became, I suppose, the one event in Britain which made The Man in The Street realize how big Rock music had become.

I'd been fractious as hell three years before about getting to Monterey, the first Rock festival in California where The Who and Hendrix, The Mamas and Papas, etc., appeared. Derek Taylor, who had been The Beatles' press officer, and had left them and set up with The Byrds in LA, beckoned me over. He knew Monterey was going to be an event. So did I, but I also had to try and convince the then features editor of the *Sunday Mirror*. Dear man, he was more into playing golf in the office. It all seemed hopeless.

But I had to get to Monterey somehow. Or somewhere close by on the West Coast of California. Right, I thought, I'll try another idea. 'Hey,' I cried, 'how about me doing a feature on Edith Head, the Hollywood costume lady, must have a million tales to tell.' 'Good one,' said the *Sunday Mirror*. Aha, I thought, my ticket to Monterey. Then: 'Sorry, we checked the files. Edith Head feature was done three years ago.'

Naturally, and to my chagrin, the *Sunday Mirror* then gave a big show to Monterey with pictures and text devoted to how 200,000 hippies hadn't got arrested and – shock, amazement – there had been no violence!

Other commitments prevented me going to the Dylan Isle of Wight Festival in '69, but the '70 one, no way was I going to miss. It was amusing, a bit, to find that Rock and Roll had become hip in the intellectual media circles. *The Grauniad* and *The Sunday Times* were preparing long critical assessments of Rock and its future. To mark its status as a National Event, the *Evening Standard* produced an Isle of Wight colour souvenir edition in their best Cup Final day style.

I approached the event in so much earnestness that I decided it should also be my holiday. We (Binks and I) secured a small cottage in Yarmouth for a week. The Isle of Wight was also a period of adjustment for us as we'd never been away together before (no, please, why don't you just hum a chorus and verse of *When I'm 64*). I discovered with a certain amount of disquiet that Binky couldn't sleep in a room without the sound of a loud clock ticking. Nor did he share my taste for plebeian pursuits like sunbathing or paddling in the sea. Were these issues to lead to incompatibility?

Previous experience of smaller outdoor festivals had shown that back-stage passes, car-park passes, coded-colour enclosure passes and, most sought-after of all, stage passes did lead to an easier festival life (even if you were just a ligger and had no business or right to be on the stage). I know this smacks of elitism, but you can't tell me that most people wouldn't prefer to grab any degree of comfort possible during those endurance marathons. Going to the lavatory back-stage in a custom-built caravan is infinitely preferable to negotiating Somme-like ditches in the open, especially in the dark and especially if you're female. Lady readers will agree that festivals tend to be spent with their legs crossed, and not for any reasons of chastity.

The festival got off to a remarkably slow start. Kris Kristofferson, then light-years away from being a superstar actor opposite Barbra Streisand, played his guitar to as many people still knocking the scaffolding stage together as he did to punters. A quaint, almost village-like atmosphere prevailed to start with. Areas of green grass, yet to be covered with sleeping bags and empty coke tins, were still visible. A Canadian band called Lighthouse, managed by one of the organizers, Rikki Farr, obligingly popped on and off and back on-stage again when it transpired that the scheduled artist had not yet arrived. Then the build-up grew at an alarming rate. For the first two or three days it had taken ten minutes in the car from our

Evening Standard

FESTIVAL FUN BOOK

Full Programme
INSIDE

24-

POP SPECIAL

Rupert Bear (very big in 1970) plays leapfrog
with his special friend Pete Townshend on
the cover of the Evening Standard's Isle of
Wight festival number.
Right: The not-too-dear cottage that we
rented in the I-o-W.

The hill at Afton Down - three days before
the festival and on the Sunday afternoon.
In between: Donovan heads backstage.

base at Yarmouth to reach the festival site at Afton Down. But as people arrived by the hundred thousand, the police routed the traffic into a vast one-way system round the island, so it took two hours now to reach the 'happenings'–as they were then called.

That festival was the biggest celebration of what was cynically called 'weekend hippiedom'. Bank clerks, building inspectors, secretaries, trainee accountants all disguised themselves in denim and covered the hillside with blue and yellow tents. Determinedly feminine young women wore long dresses and shawls–with boots–and relationships were confirmed when a drooping-moustachioed young man would introduce his companion not as his girl friend but as 'My lady'. If they'd known each other more than a month, the young man would adopt the Hell's Angels' expression and call her 'My old lady'. Gosh, that meant you were pretty well engaged!

The grassy back-stage enclosure, complete with marquee, began to take on the look of Rock and Roll's answer to the Royal Enclosure at Ascot or Smith's Lawn at Windsor. In other words, a lot of people were indulging in posturing and there were the beginnings of today's pursuit of professional posing. Eyecatching outfits and tentative outrageousness were fashionable. Who someone was no longer mattered. Enough to say that the festival had become an annual event and the goings-on back-stage at the Isle of Wight would henceforth be covered by William Hickey.

Occasionally artists would stray into this arena away from their own super inner sanctum, which can't have been a very friendly area. Melanie the folk singer told me afterwards that she'd found the festival petrifying, and saw no one there she knew. It was the prolonged waiting and the procrastination as the scheduled running order got later and later which the artists found so torturing. However, Melanie remembered just one guy who had befriended her and treated her to some hospitality in his caravan. She only discovered afterwards that it had been Keith Moon.

As the acts on-stage got more distinguished, so the enclosure in front of it got more and more crowded. Nothing was

helped by the profusion of film crews, cameramen and sound recordists linked together with their umbilical cords for sync sound, and I had a deep-rooted suspicion that not all the several hundred who crammed the Press enclosure were there to report on the festival for the world's media.

Politics had crept in and rumours were rife that an Algerian sector of the crowd wanted to 'free' the festival. Certainly some members of the public were taking matters into their own hands, and breaking down the outer fences.

We had to stand up if we wanted to see anything at all, but then the people behind us complained that they couldn't see if we stood up. We said we couldn't see anything if we didn't, so they threw cans at us anyway.

The Who went on at about three in the morning. It was very cold by then despite one's still-smelly-from-the-sheep-Afghan-de-rigueur coat. Brave Jeff Dexter, disc jockey and compere, he of the quavery voice and rimless glasses, who had been reduced earlier to tears by one bullying group manager, now sailed on-stage and announced: 'Ladies and gentlemen, a nice little band from Shepherds Bush–'The Oo'.

Townshend came on and said: 'Bloody marvellous, isn't it? We go all round the world, and come back here to play to a lot of fucking foreigners.'

We restrained the temptation to react to this, surrounded as we were by the FFs. The Who had just come back from a world tour and they had lent their PA system to the festival. All I could see from our non-vantage point under the front of the stage was Townshend's nose. Which is not as big as he thinks it is. Therefore, about three-quarters of the way through the set, I retired from the night's proceedings. No one living on the island could have slept that night. The Who were playing *Tommy,* the first time that most of the audience had heard it performed live. I could hear Daltrey's pure tones of 'Listening to you, I hear the music' across the moonlit sea, all the way back to Yarmouth Harbour.

Years later I met people who had been at the festival for vastly different reasons. One was a young doctor ministering to the druggies who had OD'd. Another was a cameraman occupying the dolly position in front of the stage for the official 'Isle of Wight' film. Yet another was Trevor Dann, a BBC producer I've been working with. For him, then a school-leaver from Nottingham, the IOW festival represented a 'dash for freedom'. 'Where were you at the Isle of Wight festival?' became one of those generation phrases like 'Where were you when Kennedy was assassinated?' A lot of Isle of Wight stories only came out later. A lot more still haven't. The financial ones were especially mysterious. All along, The Moody Blues had said they didn't want to play the festival because they were sure they wouldn't get paid; but they were persuaded into doing it and sure enough . . . they didn't get paid.

Nobody knows what happened to the considerable amount of money made over that long weekend. Though there were rumours. The film, for example, has never been shown. Whenever a festival is dismantled a certain amount of wreckage comes to light, and the Isle of Wight was surrounded by more wreckage than most.

Professional reputations were mutilated, too. Joan Baez lost a lot of folk credibility by allegedly demanding a mansion on the island to stay in, or she wouldn't go on. Joni Mitchell hit zero as far as I was concerned. An over-enthusiastic Dutch photographer jumped on the stage during her set shouting 'Smile for Amsterdam, Joni.' This ruffled

The Moody Blues - here previewed by the Evening Standard - already seem resigned to a strange conviction that they wouldn't get paid for appearing at the Isle of Wight festival. They were right. Left: A priest picnics near an impromptu altar, where Communion was celebrated on the Sunday morning. Right: Jimi Hendrix, a giant among performers, made his last major appearance at the Isle of Wight. He died the following month.

Ms Mitchell in much the same way as a bad line-call would upset Martina Navratilova at Wimbledon. 'I want some respect,' whined Joni to the photographer. First, I thought, you gotta *earn* it.

The saddest postscript to the Isle of Wight festival was that it marked the last major appearance of Jimi Hendrix. He died the following month. How he played, and what a gentle, natural man he was, has all been chronicled enough. I remember, I'd been asked to a wedding at Windsor Castle, in St George's Chapel. It was on Friday 18 September. I didn't really know why I'd been asked because I hardly knew the groom and never met the bride. Looking back, I suppose I thought: I've never been to a wedding at Windsor Castle. So I set off to drive there, alone and listening to the radio. There was a news flash – Jimi Hendrix was dead.

The wedding reception was elsewhere in Windsor. The guests were queueing in a long line. I thought: what am I doing here? I don't know anybody, and after the news I'd just heard I didn't feel like celebrating. So I just got in the car and drove around listening to the radio. Radio 1 broadcast a special tribute which, all credit to them, they had put together in just a few hours. I drove for hours around Ascot and Bracknell listening. Finding it hard to believe he was dead.

New Musical Express

EVERY FRIDAY 5p

No. 1266   Week ending May 1, 1971

WORLD'S **LARGEST** CIRCULATION OF **ANY** MUSIC PAPER

EXTRA: '208 TIMES' — 8-page supplement inside

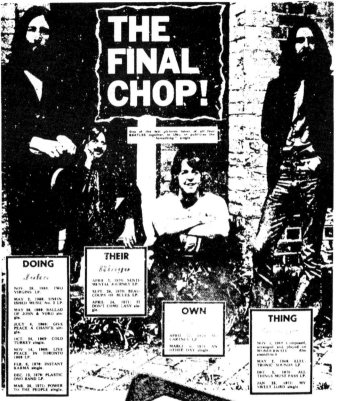

THE FINAL CHOP!

One of the best pictures taken of all four BEATLES together in 1969, to publicise the "Something" single.

NO APPEAL AGAINST TRIAL TO DISSOLVE BEATLES

THE appeal against the trial to dissolve the Beatles partnership has been dropped by George, John, Ringo and the Apple Corps Ltd. This means that fifth partner, Paul, has got his way and a receiver and manager appointed by the court will look after Beatles affairs until the present partnership is ended legally.

In simple terms, Paul is one step nearer his entire independence from a partnership that started as a friendly happening and ended as a constricting monster in his eyes.

Paul has said that he first felt the limitations of being a Beatle, tied to Apple, when he brought out his album "McCartney." In advertisements for it he was angered by the inclusion of "An Abkco-managed company" after the words Apple Records, in connection with "McCartney."

Resentment grew

His resentment grew, because he and wife Linda had done everything and Abkco, Allen Klein's company, had nothing to do with it. Yet here it was, to Paul's way of thinking, taking some sort of credit.

The question went through Paul's mind for a long time: "How do I get out?" He took legal advice and found that a court action was the only way. He went ahead.

During the hearings some nasty things were said against him by other Beatles. He didn't like them, because Paul has always been the Beatle who liked to be liked. Now he has cooled down and says he has nothing against John, George and Ringo. And he's sorry the ending had to come in a court of law, instead of maybe in a "Magical Mystery Tour" sort of explosion!

But more and more the famous four are leaving behind the word of fantasy they lived in as Beatles and becoming realists and individuals. It must be a great comfort to them to know that they can make it on their own. They don't seem to need the Beatles tag any more, although they will never lose it.

Is it good thing?

It is probably a good thing for the music business that the Beatles are now no more as a group. We have four top attractions, instead of one if financial and contractual doubts hadn't brought the legal parting, artistic ones would have. As far back as "Abbey Road" there was the feeling that the Beatles were drifting apart musically, and everyone except Ringo seems to have voiced opinions that he would quit the group.

Now the appeal against the action to break up the Beatles partnership has been dismissed. Paul is on his way to "getting out" and the others are faced with an alleged bill for some £100,000 legal fees which the judge ordered

them to pay after the first High Court hearing of 11 days.

What happens next? The court will now look into how Paul can terminate his partnership with the other partners in the Beatles. And in the meantime, Mr James Douglas Spooner, a chartered accountant and "company doctor" has been appointed by the judge, Mr Justice Stamp, to act as manager and receiver of the group's multi-million-pound businesses immediately. He would not permit the wish of John, George, Ringo and Apple Corp. Ltd. for American Allen Klein to continue as manager of their business affairs.

None of the Beatles was in court, for the five minute hearing on Monday at which the appeal was abandoned.

In announcing the decision, Lord Justice Russell said he hoped Paul and the other Beatles would reach an amicable and sensible agreement and showed himself to be with-it by ruling : "My only disappointment is that I am not unable to make a joke about preserving the Status Quo — which is the name of another pop group!"

DOING

Beatles

NOV. 29, 1968: TWO VIRGINS LP.

MAY 2, 1969: UNFINISHED MUSIC No. 2 LP.

MAY 30, 1969: BALLAD OF JOHN & YOKO single.

JULY 4, 1969: GIVE PEACE A CHANCE single.

OCT. 24, 1969: COLD TURKEY single.

NOV. 14, 1969: LIVE PEACE IN TORONTO 1969 LP.

FEB. 8, 1970: INSTANT KARMA single.

DEC. 12, 1970: PLASTIC ONO BAND LP.

MAR. 20, 1971: POWER TO THE PEOPLE single.

THEIR

Ringo

APRIL 3, 1970: SENTIMENTAL JOURNEY LP.

SEPT. 26, 1970: BEAUCOUPS OF BLUES LP.

APRIL 24, 1971: IT DON'T COME EASY single.

OWN

APRIL 17, 1970: McCARTNEY LP.

MARCH 8, 1971: AN OTHER DAY single.

THING

NOV. 1, 1968: composed, arranged and played on WONDERWALL film soundtrack.

MAY 2, 1968: ELECTRONIC SOUNDS LP.

DEC. 5, 1970: ALL THINGS MUST PASS LP.

JAN. 22, 1971: MY SWEET LORD single.

FREE

Next week
THE WO

Side A

Let it Be

Ferro Low Noise

2 × 30 min.   **C60**

The Beatles break up, and collectors strip the Apple building.

After Brian Epstein died the sharks moved in on The Beatles. It was a bit like missionaries arriving, waving bibles at some innocent South American tribe whose members were unprepared for the viruses, VD, and deadly common cold germs. Because Brian had been with them from the beginning, they hadn't been through nearly so many of the appalling rip-offs that most of their contemporaries had suffered. And therefore hadn't learnt their lessons. He had protected them, as far as his own experience had allowed, from the very worst of the Rock and Roll gangsters. So, left unprotected, they were incredibly naive. Well, some Beatles more than others. Jagger tried to warn them off an American called Allan Klein who represented The Beatles for a short while, but John was impressed that he knew the words of their songs. . . .

An urbane Aries called Peter Brown, a terribly well spoken chap, a friend of Brian's, took over as social secretary. He gave Apple its smart look – told the secretaries off if they weren't dressed well, and arranged Cordon Bleu lunches in his office, which had a sparkling log fire in winter. I don't really know what The Beatles thought of Peter. But he carried on Brian's tradition of style and elegance. Obviously he couldn't hope to control the people who were now able to get at The Beatles, and encourage their Utopian dreams. Apple really did start out like that. But then The Beatles were like haemophiliacs. If you cut their finger, you could bleed them to death. I don't think Brian could have held The Beatles together a lot longer than they existed, but now it was left to Derek Taylor, Neil Aspinall, Mal Evans – The Beatles' original roadies who were now Apple executives – and Peter to keep papering the cracks.

I began to realize just how bad the

Three phases in the life of the Fab Four.
Above: The much-loved mopheads from Liverpool.
Right: John and Yoko at the forefront of the 'Allan Klein faction' that included George (in cap) and Ringo.
Above right: Paul, now the loner who wanted Lee Eastman, Linda's father, to take over as the group's manager.

group relationship was when they recorded *Let It Be* in the basement studio at Apple. Yoko sat on the floor beside John, and no one except Billy Preston smiled. The atmosphere was very tense and hostile.

It is generally held that The Beatles broke up because John wanted Allan Klein to be their manager, persuaded George and Ringo, but not Paul. He preferred Lee Eastman, Linda's father. But there were so many other considerations. Yoko was just not accepted by the others, who had virtually grown up with John's wife, Cynthia. Mind you, she's a fascinating woman. When her liaison with John began they were inseparable. The bed-in in Amsterdam . . . the TV appearances . . . the trouble over their nude photograph together. Once I got to talk to Yoko alone. John was mixing tracks at Abbey Road Studios, one of the few tasks she obviously couldn't involve herself in. I thought she would be the clichéd Oriental inscrutable. She turned out to be very communicative, very scrutable! Her worst fear, she said, was to end up an old woman 'shaking', living alone in a high-rise New York apartment.

Also John, Paul and George were finding it increasingly difficult to get as much of their own material recorded on Beatles' albums as they wanted. The Lennon-McCartney writing team had long since ceased being a partnership and an obvious diversity in styles had appeared. It's clear which are John's terse acerbic songs on the 'White Album'—and on *Abbey Road* Paul's simpler melodic songs were *his* own work. Then again George, frustrated for so many years as a writer by the Lennon-McCartney domination, needed to show the world he could write classic songs like *Something*.

Apple wasn't a place, it was an experience. I believe they really intended it to work like a dream factory. Their dreams had worked—they were the four most famous people in the world—so why not help other people achieve their ambitions? The trouble was, they never realized just how many people there are in the world with unrealized dreams. And people *came* from all over the world to seek their fortunes via the Fab Four. The Beatles were used, abused, misused, pursued, pleaded with. Poets, astrologers, songwriters, musicians, painters,

photographers, designers—they all wrote to Apple, phoned or turned up on the doorstep at Savile Row. The Beatles were able to help a few, but very few.

Derek Taylor's assistant was Richard di Lello, the American 'house hippy' as he was called. He poured the drinks and rolled the spliffs, smiled a lot and never said a word. Obviously he was memorizing everything that happened, and going home and writing it all down. He wrote a beautiful book afterwards about Apple, called *The Longest Cocktail Party*. It *was* a huge cocktail party until I inadvertently got Richard fired by writing a thoughtless piece about the demise of Apple, and quoted Richard. This was just the chance Klein, who by now had taken over, was waiting for. Di Lello and my long-standing secretary friend, Carol, were got rid of.

If you were famous, of course, it was easier to gain access through the famous front door (no graffitti on it then, Peter Brown would have had it removed each morning!). Ken Kesey would sit quietly beaming. Lauren Bacall came in because her children wanted to meet The Beatles.

Even their Christmas party was a disaster. It was to be for children. John and

BED
PEACE.

HAIR
PEACE.

Scenes of Love, Peace, the
Amsterdam bed-in . . . and
John and Yoko as Father
and Mother Christmas at
the party that took a
downhill turn when Hell's
Angels from San Francisco
took over.

'All we are saying is
give peace a chance'.

John Lennon 1940–1980

While this book was being printed
John Lennon was shot down on a
street in New York.

Years after The Beatles broke up rumours of reunions persisted. When Wings put on Rockaria most of London was convinced that 'this would be it'. But it wasn't.
Below: John Lennon's live musical pursuits were via The Plastic Ono Band, though he and Yoko were not ever-presents in the line-up.

BEATLES

ABBEY ROAD N

Side One
COME TOGETHER
SOMETHING
MAXWELL'S SILVER HAMMER
OH! DARLING
OCTOPUS'S GARDEN
I WANT YOU (She's so heavy)

Side Two
HERE COMES THE SUN
BECAUSE
YOU NEVER GIVE ME YOUR MONEY
SUN KING
MEAN MR MUSTARD
POLYTHENE PAM
SHE CAME IN THROUGH THE BATHROOM WINDOW
GOLDEN SLUMBERS
CARRY THAT WEIGHT
THE END

Apple Records

An E.M.I. recording
Photographs by Iain
Printed by Garrod

mono

PARLOPHONE · EMI · BEATLES FOR SALE

LONG PLAY 33⅓ R.P.M. · E.M.I. RECORD
HAYES · MIDDLESE

Produced by GEORGE MARTIN

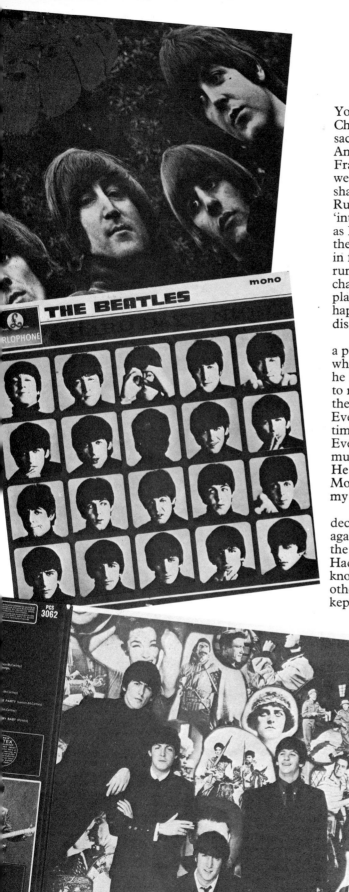

Yoko dressed up as Father and Mother Christmas and dispensed presents out of a sack. All well and good. But then the Hell's Angels moved in. They'd come from San Francisco and 'occupied' the building for weeks. The party ended in violence and shambles and stealing. The sequence in The Rutles film—a rather in-joke where Eric Idle 'interviews' George Harrison who is dressed as Derek Taylor—was true in essence. Behind the two of them, who are purporting to stand in front of the Apple building, people are running in and out, blatantly removing desks, chairs, plants, office equipment, record players. It was a bitter joke, because that *had* happened. Cars the Beatles 'owned', disappeared. So did the odd house.

On New Year's Eve 1969 Ringo threw a party at his house in North London to which Peter Brown invited me. I don't think he had consulted Ringo on this point, much to my embarrassment. George Harrison was there, as were Klaus Voorman, Kenny Everett, Michael Caine and Lulu, still at that time married to Bee Gee Maurice Gibb. Everett, always a shy person, hid in a corner muttering 'God, they're all so FAMOUS!' He then began a rumour that the Queen Mother was coming. Lulu believed him. 'Och, my mother would be so thrilled,' she cooed.

The irony of the evening was that Paul decided at that point to initiate legislation against the other three. This was the end of the Fab Four. The story broke the next day. Had the *Daily Sketch*, my then employers, known that I was at a party with two of the other Beatles, I don't think I would have kept my job much longer.

Memorabilia from the happier days when The Beatles and their music changed the lives of millions - including mine.

Polaroid
Snapshots

I WANT TO GET OUT OF THIS BEATLE TRAP, SAYS PAUL

PAUL McCARTNEY talked at his hideaway home yesterday about his rift with John Lennon.

NIGEL BENSON

The bearded tousle-haired Beatle said: "I dig John. There is a rift, but it's not a bad one. I just want to get out of this trap."

McCartney has started an action to dissolve the Beatles' partnership. "I suppose it ceased to be a working partnership eight months ago. I left in June," he said.

"Song-writing between John and I came to a halt

a year ago, but the Beatles' partnership goes on for seven more years and this is why I want out now.

"The other three of them could sit down now and write me out of the group. I would be quite happy.

"I could pick up my cash and get out.

"I don't know how much

is involved, but I don't want Allen Klein as my manager."

On his future he said: "I am just going to write songs — and they will be better than ever. I have got an album ready for release now."

ANNE NIGHTINGALE writes: The three remaining Beatles show no signs of splitting amongst themselves and Ringo told me last night: "George will probably produce my next album. He's really in production!"

CHEERFUL

George and Ringo are probably the closest friends of the three Beatles left. A common interest in music is the obvious reason.

John, George and Ringo use each other as "session" men during their recordings — each one taking a back seat for the other.

The general atmosphere at Apple since Paul quit has been one of cheerful resignation.

The Beatles always liked things out in the open.

Left: Paul confirms the fatal break from his 'hideaway farm'. Opposite: Polaroid snapshots tell the world that the new partnerships – with Linda and Wings - are alive and kicking.

Beatle Paul with his wife on his hideaway farm.

But it was an unwritten law that if you once blew a confidence on The Beatles they were unremittingly unforgiving. Yet I don't think any of them liked the crawlers. They didn't mind open criticism – of their music, a newly grown beard, or their opinions. But, being The Beatles, they were betrayed by 'friends' so many times.

Anyway it couldn't have lasted for ever. And to all those who kept clamouring for any reunions, I would say: just be glad that The Beatles *were*. I still believe they changed the lives of millions–including mine. So thanks, John, Paul, George and Ringo.

Each Sunday afternoon the students tried to rule, and very nearly succeeded, but they had not reckoned with the insidious power of Apathy . . .

Right after the Sunday request show came to an end at the close of 1979, I had a card written to *Mailbag*, saying 'Dear Annie, Why?–Puzzled, Leeds.'

And that said it all. No one will admit it openly, but it was Leeds Uni. that killed off the request show–with a little help from Hull, Bath, Keele, St Andrews, Aberystwyth, Warwick, Trent Poly, North Staffs Poly, Nottingham Uni., Keble, Birmingham Art College and dear Heriot Watt Uni. in Edinburgh. The students just moved in and 'occupied' the show. People would even write in to the 'Leeds University Request Show'. They were witty, inventive and they asked for good records–which is why their records got played. The elitism of it did worry me, especially when someone else wrote in saying, 'I don't go to Leeds University so I suppose you won't play a record for me . . .'

My theory about why we got so many requests from students is this: who else is sitting listening to the radio on a Sunday afternoon with a piece of paper and a pen in front of them? They were all supposed to be working! I was constantly accused: 'If I fail my exams it will be your fault.'

They'd do anything to gain attention. Write in on a rubber glove, a banana skin, House of Commons notepaper, loo paper (obviously); I had a brick once with a request on it, and an engraved message on an unidentified piece of motor bike.

It was like a club, I suppose. We had our own language. Like NTNTM–which was shorthand for Names Too Numerous To Mention. Some people would write in every week, like Hilda Stark of Upper Popplewell. A chap called Philip in Maidenhead, Berkshire won the highly difficult Daisy Chain competition about half a dozen times. Regency Stephen used to write in for his Mum, Regency Dorothy. And she'd reciprocate. A young lady called Mandy invited me for Christmas to her mum's farm in the West Country. I never met any of these people but obviously they felt like close friends. The feedback was fantastic. One chance throwaway remark–and the following week there would be a shoal of letters. They'd tease me, propose marriage and issue threats. Those cards used to start: 'Now look here Nightingale, unless you play . . . we will converge on the BBC with a sack full of rats/our landlady's eccles cakes/a plague of frogs.'

Sometimes I'd meet them at gigs. They'd come up and say things like: 'Do you remember me? I was the one who dared you to say Brest on the radio because I was studying there.'

The most difficult to deal with were those who would beg 'PLEASE PLEASE PLEASE . . .' literally a thousand times on several sheets of paper, and then at the end they'd ask for some really awful record. What do you do? I wanted to keep all the letters and cards we ever had, with a sort of hopeless optimism that one day we'd get around to playing a record for everyone that ever wrote in. Quite impossible of course.

Then there would be the 'phoney' cards. Usually they would request a very very new record, and be written by record company personnel. Bernie Andrews, my producer, had an inbuilt ability to spot the phoney ones. If he was suspicious he'd check addresses in Kelly's Directory, or even phone people up.

Some cards were particularly distressing. One came for a young girl in the very last stages of terminal cancer. Her husband asked me not to read the details on the air–I think he explained the severity of the situation just so that Bernie and I would

Me in the studio, plus a listener's subtle reminder that Bernie Andrews, my producer, deserved his share of credit too - especially since his duties included carrying the can when things went adrift (see also page 54).

Overpage: Samples from the mail. This particular week it was Debbie Day. I'd also celebrated Sharon Sunday and special occasions for Trevors and Nigels. Cards were colour-coded so that I could pick up the essential bits, e.g. green for sender, pink for dedication, yellow for record. Yes, it does work!

ANNE NIGHTINGALE (sorry)
THE BERNIE ANDREWS REQUEST SHOW
RADIO ONE
B.B.C.
LONDON W1A 4WW

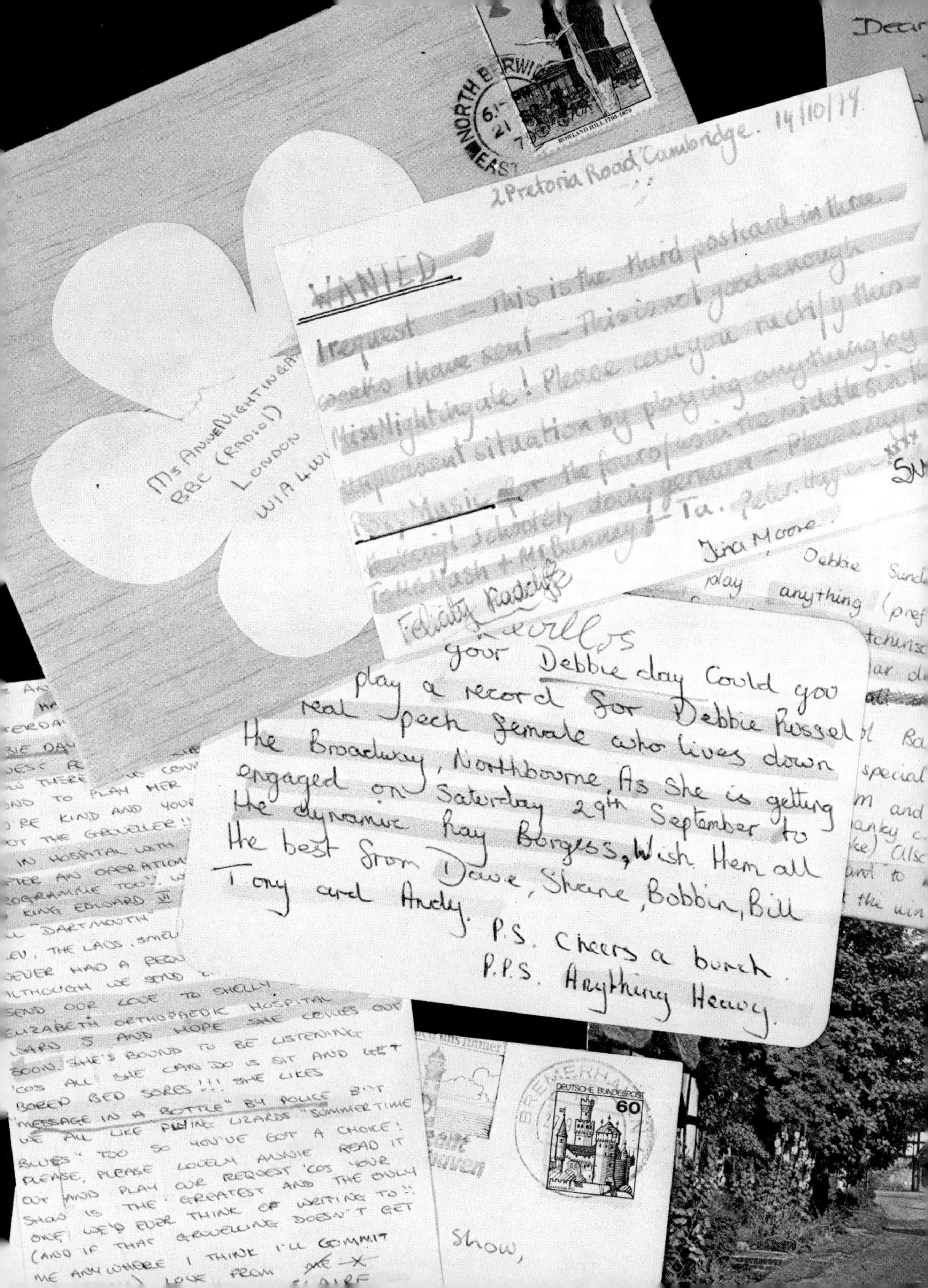

Envelope postmark: NORTH BERWICK EAST 6.15 PM 21 7 [ROWLAND HILL 1795-1879]

2 Pretoria Road, Cambridge. 14/10/74.

Ms Annie (Nightingale?)
BBC (Radio 1)
London
W1A 1WW

WANTED — This is the third postcard in three
I request — This is not good enough
weeks I have sent — can you rectify this
Miss Nightingale! Please can you rectify this
unpleasant situation by playing anything by...
Rock Music — for the four of us in the middle sin th..
Hendersey's school doing german — Please say o..
To Nash + McBurney — Ta. Peter Hay...

Tina Moore.
Felicity Radcliffe

Neville's
your Debbie day Could you
play a record for Debbie Russel of
real pech female who lives down
the Broadway, Northbourne. As she is getting
engaged on Saterday 29th September to
the dynamic hay Borgess, Wish them all
the best from Dave, Shane, Bobbin, Bill
Tony and Andy.
P.S. Cheers a bunch.
P.P.S. Anything Heavy.

...TERDA..
...SIE DAY
...EST R..
W THERE IS COMM..
OND TO PLAY HER..
J'RE KIND AND YOUR
OT THE GROVELLER!!
IN HOSPITAL WITH
TER AN OPERATION
ROGRAMME TOO!! W
KING EDWARD VII
L DARTMOUTH
EV. THE LADS, SMEL
DEVER HAD A REQU
ALTHOUGH WE SEND
SEND OUR LOVE TO SHELLY
ELIZABETH ORTHOPAEDIC HOSPITAL
WARD 5 AND HOPE SHE COMES OUT
SOON. SHE'S BOUND TO BE LISTENING
'COS ALL SHE CAN DO IS SIT AND GET
BORED BED SORES !!! SHE LIKES
"MESSAGE IN A BOTTLE" BY POLICE BUT
WE ALL LIKE FLYING LIZARDS "SUMMERTIME
BLUES" TOO! SO YOU'VE GOT A CHOICE!
PLEASE, PLEASE LOVELY ANNIE READ IT
OUT AND PLAY OUR REQUEST 'COS YOUR
SHOW IS THE GREATEST AND THE ONLY
ONE! WE'D EVER THINK OF WRITING TO!!
(AND IF THAT GROVELLING DOESN'T GET
ME ANYWHERE I THINK I'LL COMMIT
) LOVE FROM ME X
CLAIRE

Envelope postmark: BREMERHAVEN DEUTSCHE BUNDESPOST 60

Show,

must be bad if I have
a request to you myself,
self!! Please play a record
own choice (preferably not Punk
th birthday on 4th October,
mention everyone in Collegians
ball club, especially, Reggie,
Jonty + Dawy + Robert; also
Elizabeth, Alison, Evelyn, Karen,
e play this for me.
z Courtney, 6, Deramore Drive 9
Belfast 9

thought that being as it is
I could chance a reque
how Co written to
ads Fleetwood succe

Dear Anne,
Could you mention I
WILLIAMS of Badgers Close, Ches
Green, Shirley, Solihull, please, in you
special 'DEBS DAY' programme. Sh
is a dizzy redhead, who will be
eighteen on Nov 9th and is getting
engaged to my son Martin on Nov 10th.
She's full of fun and I look forward
to having her as a daughter-in-law.
Thanking you.
Yours Sincerely
Valerie Hall.

WHERE IN BAKEWELL
DERBYSHIRE

th September 1979)
record) by Deb
Bakewell) becos
ts, also blue

girls, boys and
to Brucie-Baby
an(Hope he gets
didn't go to last
lease', love to
LEASE) tell
ush himself do

that yet
We've been
Light and a half
and

Dear Anne, Buggles * And not "mod" (Yuck!
idea. The Debbie I know is a long suffering
least, she makes out, she is!) Nurse. She (Miss
in the Eastbourne area!) would like anything i
Top 40 or so. For myself, could you *make it
more radical (e.g NOT disco rubbish!) Please
you devote it, also, to Carl (her boyfriend
all 3rd year Chemists at Imperial college (don
University) - Thank God it's almost over! (don
And dedicate it to anyone I've yours
forgotten due to Happy (Kemp.) P.S Carl sorry
chronic lack of brain! a literary
but what do
for sunday af

Dear Annie,

I shall be extremely grateful if you will play a record f
on your 'Deborah' spot, she is Deb Cousins, 11 Elwyn Court,
who is feeling a bit miserable at the moment and I'm sure
up no end, her favourite groups are Status Quo, Sant
Thanking you in anticipation.
from,

understand. He wanted us to play her favourite record, which was not one we'd ordinarily play. It was a very difficult moment, but I heard from a relative afterwards that the girl had died the same day her request was played.

There were, however, lots of running jokes through the show. A guy at Southampton University founded the International Apathy League, and sent me a badge. He wrote: 'I would have written before but, you know, I couldn't be bothered.' The IAL was well under way when the Organization Against Apathy got going from its headquarters in Worcester. They challenged the IAL to meet them—but, of course, got no reply. Well, not for a long time.

I conducted other get-togethers by radio. Trying to find boyfriends for a group of schoolgirls in Bournemouth, who were prepared to be met, in traditional style, behind the bicycle sheds. And there was a lonely bloke in Manchester who wanted to meet girls at a particular time at a particular bus stop. One does what one can!

The most effective piece of audience participation came a few weeks after I began a new Rock show on Friday nights in 1980. I had been interviewing Joe Strummer of The Clash, at the time when their single *London Calling* had reached No 15 in the Chart. 'It'll go Top Ten without a doubt,' I assured him. Joe was dubious. 'Bet you ANYTHING,' I said enthusiastically. 'OK,' he said, 'a Cadillac.'

The following week the record went up four places to No 11. My confidence in its progress was maintained. In the next week's Chart *London Calling* DROPPED. So now I owed Joe Strummer a Cadillac. I explained my plight during the radio show. Ten minutes later, the technical operator

took a phone call to the studio. Over the talk-back from his control booth he said: 'Chap on the phone says he's got a Cadillac you can have.'

Very funny, very amusing. I called the chap back, expecting to deal with a nutter. His name was Terry Laverty and he was serious. 'Joe didn't bet you a new Cadillac, did he? Right, well I've got a '68 model I don't want any more.'

I was overjoyed. A special presentation was to be made outside Broadcasting House, when Terry would hand over his white Cadillac to me, and I would then hand it over to The Clash. While this was being arranged I told Pete Townshend, a great Clash fan, the story so far. 'It'll never happen,' he said. 'You'll never get the car. I bet you a Rolls Royce.'

Presentation day arrived—with a frantic phone call from Terry. 'You won't believe this,' he said, 'but the Cadillac broke down outside the pub last night.' By now we had a full corps of Press photographers and a film crew from *Nationwide* waiting. But Terry, despite the fact he'd also lost his job the previous day, was not a man to renegue on a promise. He hired a transporter to pick up the stricken Cadillac from Surrey and drive it in to London. It's as well that the Caddy was not functioning. Joe Strummer couldn't drive, but he had intended nevertheless to leap behind the wheel and roar through the West End in it. In fact The Clash hit on a better plan. They had just been playing in the Steel-strike-hit town of Corby, and were so appalled by the plight of the Steelworkers that they donated the Cadillac to the Confederation of Steelworkers to be raffled. A noble gesture. And, by the way Pete, where's the Rolls Royce?

Then there were the badges. In the '60s people may have said it with flowers, but in the '70s and early '80s the badge was the message. I could have opened a shop, thanks to the constant deluge from listeners and the ever-eager record companies. Right: Typical mildly threatening postcard, this time from a 10cc fan.

O.K. Nightingale, I suppose you thought it was great sport to ridicule me in front of millions, make an example of me. Well I hope you enjoyed it. They say being thick stems from lack of education not lack of intelligence so I shan't call you brainless. But you see one does not send in a request for THE WITCHES OF DEAN ROW HIGH SCHOOL and then supply an address so they can hop on their broomsticks and beat the living daylights out of me. Up to now I have been involved in 2 kidnappings, 1 water bomb fight and 1 flour fight and a very active propoganda war. I am top of the witches wanted list — home is the only safe place, I can't have my address to everyone revealing my name + address witheld. GET A 10cc TRACK FOR THE W.K.P.F.O.

The ex-reporter-turned-broadcaster ventures out as an 'entertainer' on the gig circuit.

I did my first gig on 1 May 1970. It was the day I started writing my diary. The gig was at a Young Farmers' do at Wincanton Race Course in the West Country. They wanted solid, unsophisticated pop and it was the first time I'd ever stood up in front of an audience and been paid as an entertainer.

I didn't have a *clue*. As I pointed out to myself afterwards, one clearly cannot just murmur into a mike, as one does at the Beeb. Not to 600 tipsy farmers weaving sweatily about clutching pints of frothing ale. I think I should be grateful now that they didn't throw me off the stage.

Being a 'live' DJ is halfway between being the conjuror at a kids' party and the MC at a works' Christmas outing. You've got to keep control and keep smiling. No one would book me for years because promoters didn't think a girl/female/woman could cope with an audience. Now I don't find it difficult. I just get a bit schoolmistressy if the audience grows too bouncy.

There's no doubt I must have been pretty tacky to begin with. An ex-newspaper-reporter-turned-broadcaster doth not necessarily a good entertainer make. At a club in Coventry the manager dragged me off the stage after ten minutes and said I was so awful he was going to pay me off with a very small percentage of my fee. I was so lacking in confidence that I woefully agreed. I only found out later than he'd done or tried to do the same thing to Noel Edmonds the week before.

When I started doing gigs it was mainly at Mecca dance halls which had been transformed into huge discos. The managers were all left over from a previous era. They would impress one in their office about how Frank Sinatra was a 'personal friend' (how can you be an impersonal friend?). Their de-rigueur outfit was always the same. A midnight blue, slightly shiny tuxedo worn over a white nylon dress-shirt, edged with navy-blue broderie anglaise nylon frills, and a too-large teddy-bearish velvet bow tie. They would delight in telling me: 'We 'ad Paul Burnett last week, 'e pulled in twelve 'undred.' This was usually said in a venomous tone because the audience for my appearance numbered something like 350.

But gradually I broke into the college circuit, which was much more fun because, most important of all, I didn't have to play disco music. The problem of being a 'celebrity' (ugh!) DJ is that half the audience wants you to play the music you play on the radio. The other half couldn't care less who you are, and just want to dance to the latest by the Detroit Spinners. So you can't win!

I've always travelled alone to the venues and used borrowed equipment. What's the sense in dragging a huge road show around? People don't applaud a PA system – or not at the places I've ever been to. But I've always taken my own records and insisted on playing only them. This is a problem if I am travelling by train. I go through a heart-wrenching process before leaving home of what to take and what to leave behind. Leave out Wreckless Eric, and what will they ask for? Assume the resident DJ will have the playable singles in the Top Twenty – and he hasn't.

Then, of course, one must take goodies: Radio One sunshields, diaries, calendars, badges and T-shirts. Plus giveaway albums, cassettes and singles. Because of record company inefficiency I often get two or three of the same single or album. In this way the records I give out to the audience *can* be of quite a reasonable nature. Well, *I* think so. Lately, though, ungrateful punters have been handing or indeed *throwing* them back at me!

Fortunately, around '77, my musical taste and music for dancing began to mesh. At last I could play 'credible' music and not leave half the audience disgruntled. But even then promoters tried to stop me playing punk. They seemed to think that punk equalled instant violence. Well, I've never instigated violence – nor have I ever been gobbed on.

Radio One DJs of the mid-'70s. Not many people remember this, but Terry Wogan was a Radio One jock. Along with David Hamilton and Ed Stewart. I'm glad Terry Wogan went. He used to make me laugh so much on handovers that I couldn't speak for minutes after. Right: Assortment of Radio One goodies that listeners could buy or, better still, be given by a visiting DJ on a gig.

BBC Radio 1 Goodies
PO Box 275, Portishead, Bristol, BS20 9SG

I'm a great believer in singalongs, and audience participation. A great standby is the Albertos' satirical record *Heads Down No Nonsense Mindless Boogie*. I invite members of the audience to be star head-bangers. If they can't find a convenient wall, they can use the floor to bang their heads on. This game was put to great effect at St Edmund Hall, Oxford University, at a May Ball, where my resident DJ and slave for the evening was Sir Winston Churchill's grandson, Rupert Soames. Now there's a good potential DJ if ever I met one—and I met him crawling under a table to get to the record decks. The undergraduates of St Edmund Hall who, I must say, looked all very sexy in their dinner-jackets, threw themselves into the head-banging competition with great enthusiasm. After a few minutes one came up to me proudly pointing out a gash in his noble forehead. 'Look,' he said, 'Real BLOOD.' Satisfyingly, it had a distinct blue tinge.

Having said I don't invoke violence, this

At a St Valentine's Day dance at RAF Abingdon I thought they'd want romance and took boxes of heart-shaped confetti; but the airmen, certified headbangers all, demanded constant Quo (below).

does not rule out blood-letting. At RAF Abingdon, I was to be hostess at a St Valentine's Day dance. I imagined a romantic evening of pilots and WRAFs wrapping themselves around each other, canoodling, swopping eternity rings in case tomorrow it would be 'Scramble!' at dawn, or whatever is the current phrase.

Not a bit of it. Firstly there were almost no girls in sight, and secondly RAF Abingdon wanted Status Quo, Status Quo, and more Status Quo. I'd spent all that day buying heart-shaped confetti, and prettily packed boxes of heart-shaped chocolates. Oh well . . . About halfway through the evening a young man pushed past the security to ask for my autograph.

'Later, later,' I said, riffling through my record box without looking up.

'No, I gotta have it now, I'm going to hospital.'

To prove his point he held up his right hand which was covered with blood.

'What happened?' I asked.

'Well,' he replied, 'I was the first person to shout out the right answer when you asked the name of the bass player in Public Image, and you said come round the back and collect your prize.'

This indeed was true, but the unfortunate airman had gone too far round the back, had ended up outside my locked dressing-room door, pounded on it and put his hand through a large glass panel.

But then one does collide with human nature at these get-togethers. Rhyl in North Wales is an unforgettable place for me. I drove there alone for a gig, and thanks to the AA who gave me a route map ignoring all motorways the journey took eight hours and I arrived late, tired and extremely agitated. There had been a band playing earlier who were less than amused that one of the audience had entertained himself throughout their set by shaking up bottles of Lanson Black Label champagne and exploding the contents all over their equipment.

The members of the band were telling me this at the bar of the hotel where the gig was—and where I was staying that night. The champagne shaker then came up and began to talk to me. He informed me that he was Leo Sayer's manager—an unfortunate ploy as Leo Sayer's manager was (and is) Adam Faith, whom I knew very well. My raised eyebrows no doubt indicated that I didn't believe him.

'Well I'm his producer,' he offered.

'Oh, really. And how is Tel?' I asked. (Adam's real name is Terry Nelhams, and Tel is his nickname.)

However, no amount of frostiness was to deter Champagne Charlie. It transpired that he was about 22, had been left two million pounds by his father the previous year and was obviously hell-bent on becoming a bankrupt as soon as possible. He had flown from the Isle of Man with a few friends including a bemused taxi-driver. To my horror I learned that the whole party was also staying at the same hotel. And had stayed before. Because of the young man's 'generosity', he was a valued customer.

Gradually the occupants of the bar began to disappear and I asked the old retainer of a night porter, the only remaining member of the hotel staff, for my room key. Champagne Charlie grabbed it out of his hand, and whisked my suitcase up the stairs. When I arrived at the room he was comfortably sprawled on the bed.

'I'm staying here,' he said. 'There's a girl in my room, but I don't like her.'

I pointed out that that was his problem and would he please leave as I was desperately tired and wanted to go to sleep. Champagne Charlie said no, he wouldn't move. He wanted to talk to me.

'Right,' I said, 'I'm going to get the manager.'

Downstairs I told the retainer: 'There's a man in my room. Get him out.'

When the retainer discovered who it was, he almost literally quaked and said: 'Oh, I can't move him, no.'

The manager of the hotel had gone. 'I tell you what,' said the retainer helpfully. 'You hide in the lounge, and I'll see what I can do.'

OK, it was dumb to agree to such a charade but it was now four o'clock in the morning and I was prepared to go along with anything that would result in sleep. The retainer crept off carrying a master key. The lounge remained in pitch darkness until soon after dawn. Then lights flooded on, and I woke up to find myself staring down the snout of a cleaning lady's Hoover. I thought, I can't beat this lot, I can't join them, either. I quit town.

My innocent ears fail me, and Mick Jagger puts one past the BBC.

Mick Jagger seems to have lost all his notoriety nowadays. Pity. I can see him at 70, a Cecil Beaton-like figure, leading a genteel, very comfortable existence. I like Mick, always have. He's ruthless, has infinite strength, can be very compassionate, and loves kids. This last is a quality he hasn't always wanted to publicize.

On one early occasion when I interviewed Mick, he was practising the Jagger put-down tactic. This is employed with the most magnificent insolence. I recognized it as exactly the sort I used to practise at school on Miss Durston, my domestic science teacher. You don't say anything, just stare – aggressively. Jagger would do this having already tried to throw you off balance by snapping out: 'Well, what do you want to know then?' The faint-hearted interviewer finds that every burning question he ever wanted to ask Mick Jagger has just flown out of his mind. It very nearly threw me on this occasion, as I adopt a risky interview technique at the best of times (this is to say I haven't a clue what I'm going to ask my prey till the moment arrives).

But I was not going to be intimidated, so I didn't ask him anything. 'I'll just carry on reading this fan mail then,' he said. At this time Mick was still living with Marianne Faithfull, and effectively bringing up her son Nicholas.

Gradually I drew out of Mick his attitude towards children. He told me how the boy would wind Marianne round his little finger, but that Mick could control him by the tone of his voice. I'd never heard Jagger talking about child care before. This was just what I wanted, some different aspect to him that he hadn't revealed before. Suddenly he realized the image was slipping. 'What is all this baby-coddling about, anyway,' he said, jumping out of his chair. But it was too late.

Typical Jagger insolence (right) though in his years with Marianne Faithfull (together, below) he talked to me with surprising tenderness about his feelings towards children.

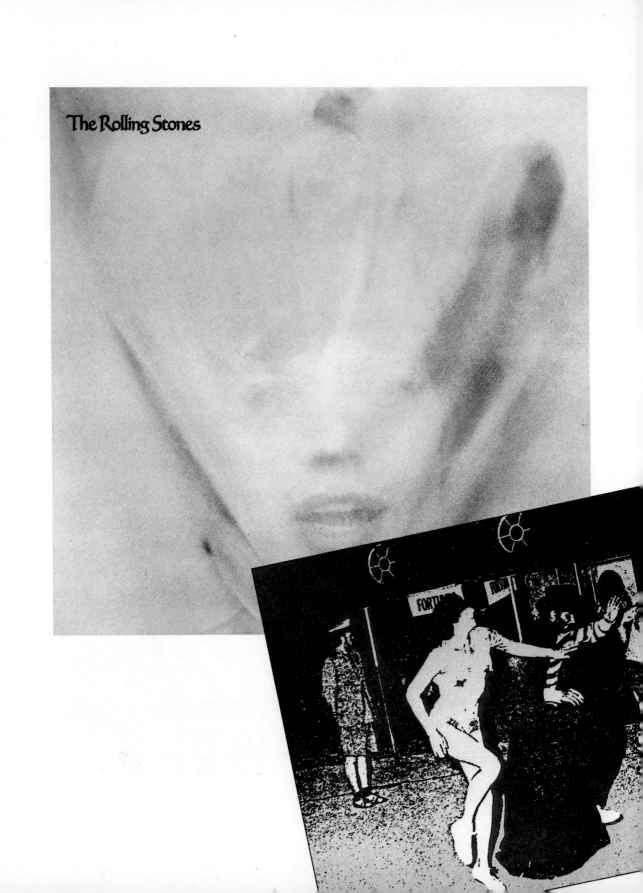

Above: Mick Superstar has a word or two with Princess Margaret.
Left: Strange goings-on at Blenheim Palace, where a grand launch was held for Goat's Head Soup, the album with the fateful Starfucker track.
Opposite: Album cover for Goat's Head Soup.

The real fun with Jagger started after the release of *Goat's Head Soup* in 1973. At that time I was doing a Wednesday late-evening review programme with Alan Black on Radio One. With the producer Bernie Andrews we'd get together during the day, and put together a running order for that night's show. I had just come back from France and hadn't read any advance publicity for the new Stones album. And as luck would have it, Alan had just gone to France and I was to do the show on my own with Bernie. I sat in his office and listened alone and attentively to *Goat's Head Soup*. While I was playing a track called *Star Star*, another producer, Jeff Griffin, known for his deadpan humour, put his head round the door and said: 'Going to play that track tonight, then?'

'Well, yes, I think so. It sounds like one of the best tracks on the album – I like the Chuck Berry riff.'

Jeff didn't know that I didn't know. The fact that *Star Star* was actually Mick singing 'Starfucker' all the way through the song. Over and over again. Once you *knew* – and everyone else at Radio One did – then you could hear the words as clear as day. But, blissfully ignorant, as was Bernie who also listened to the track, and who carries the can for what goes out on air – I played the track that night.

The following evening there was a big party for The Stones at Blenheim Palace – well it was in the cafeteria, actually, and the place was stripped of any valuables. Mick and Bianca swep' in, both in white, to much clicking of shutters.

After a bit I said hallo to Mick and told him I'd been playing some tracks from the album the night before.

'Oh, which ones?' he said.

I mentioned a couple of others and *Star Star*.

He double-took. 'You played WHA-AT?'

Mick immediately rounded up other Stones and said: 'Hey, she played *Star Star*. We'll give you a special prize.'

Bear in mind I still didn't know what all the fuss was about. But it was nice having all this attention. I then bounced up to Teddy Warwick, the executive producer of our programme, who carries even more of the

can than the producer, and told him how pleased Mick was that I'd played *Star Star*.

To my surprise he also said: 'You played WHAA-AT?' but with a slightly different intonation. Slowly, gradually, as in a fog, I remembered a review in *NME* that day of The Stones album in which a track called *Starfucker* was mentioned. Funny, I had thought, I don't recall the song. Now the full horrible truth hit me.

It also hit the Controller of Radio One who summoned Bernie Andrews to his office for an explanation. In fact their paths failed to cross and Bernie had to wait two weeks before being 'carpeted'. He didn't waste time though. Bernie's point was that it had been a mistake anyone could make. To prove this he dragged strangers in off the street where he lives and asked them to identify the words in *Star Star*. Some of them came up with *extraordinary* phrases that weren't in the song at all.

The BBC took a very serious view of *Star Star*, partly because unfortunately it wasn't the first time the Wednesday review programme had played 'dubious' tracks. There had been the matter of *Souvenir of London* by Procol Harum, which turned out to be about VD. And one night we'd been unable to find a particular edited version of a Steely Dan track, and played, by mistake, the unexpurgated track.

So all in all we were under deep suspicion. What really helped our cause was the fact that BBC TV News had also played *Star Star* over a news item about The Stones being back in London.

When I saw Mick afterwards he never failed proudly to congratulate me on playing *Starfucker* on BBC radio. I just never had the heart to tell him that it was all a rather dumb mistake.

Right: While we're on the subject of Jaggerisms, how would you like one of these through your letterbox? (From an Earl's Court concert.)

Overpage: Some of the memorabilia which has rained in on my house during a decade or more - from albums and badges to scarves, T-shirts, ties, stationery sets, balloons and clocks.

Side A — Keith Moon

Ferro
Low
Noise

2 x 30 min. C60

Premier

THE WHO

Portrait of an express train.

It didn't seem important at the time, but I had the pleasure of introducing The Who on their first television appearance. They were not in the studio, but on what must have been one of the first-ever promotional films specially made for a single. The record was *I Can't Explain* and it was made by Kit Lambert, son of the conductor Constant Lambert, who was one of The Who's first managers. His partner was Chris Stamp, brother of actor Terence Stamp. I was doing a TV Request Show and I can remember interviewing members of the audience who asked for The Who, and had been fans since the band first formed under the name The High Numbers.

I interviewed them at various intervals during the Sixties, as a matter of course, along with the Beatles, Stones, Kinks, Hollies, Herman's Hermits, Animals and the rest. Their visual image was always different. The Pop Art look, Pete's Union Jack jacket, Roger's extraordinary blond hair. And gradually their personalities began to emerge. Pete was leapt on by the media, because he was articulate. He admitted taking drugs on a BBC TV programme called *Whole Scene Going*. He'd write long letters to *Melody Maker*. He was biting, critical – and he was writing songs for other young men who wanted to come home all covered in blood and who hoped they'd die before they got old. Moon was only beginning to get his reputation as ace prankster. His initial image was pretty pop star.

He married Kim Kerrigan, a model from Bournemouth, when she was 16. In the

Moon with fellow-Who members exhibits his progression from pretty if aggressive Mod to the ace prankster with satanic overtones. Here in embryo is the legendary destroyer of hotel rooms, the all-night crumpet chaser, the mugger of phoney vicars . . . and the hero of numerous other outrages ascribed to him which he probably did not commit. Such is the fate of most high-quality hell-raisers.

Rock and Roll tradition, this was kept a secret as it was considered detrimental to a pop group if any of its members was married. Kim would answer the phone and pretend to be Keith's sister. Suspicious fans would nevertheless wait outside their home and attack Kim. Keith on one occasion chased them off with an axe. It's probably quite well known that The Who combined all the ancient Four Elements: Roger, Water; Pete, Earth; Keith, Fire—what else?—and John, Air.

What was so important about The Who was their passion for The Who. I don't think The Beatles believed in and loved the Whole

nearly as much as The Who did, and hopefully still do. Each one of them would subjugate himself for the sake of this four-part creation. Interdependence makes great bands. Clearly Pete always felt he needed Roger to do full justice to his songs. Roger doesn't write so he needed Pete. Moon, who hated drum solos, needed the others and John was needed to be Mr Darkness and create those reliable but original bass patterns. What has always been so great, so different about The Who is their unwillingness to Cover Up. If there's a row between the band everyone knows it—the roadies, the audience, friends, the Press. The

Who's passion and their old-style violence are interwoven. To see them after a gig was in some ways the only way to understand what they'd put into it.

Adrenalin seems to affect the eyes. They'd all stare straight through you blankly. Roger has said things to me after a gig—and been unable to recall them later: 'I never know what I'm doing or saying after I come off-stage.' Peter seems to do a mental prowl round and round echoing his own stage act. As for Mooney, well, we'll come to him later.

Admittedly other Rock bands are known to have a cup of hot chocolate and go quietly to bed after a gig—but with The Who

Beneath the   drag or gold lame was a frenetic drummer who took hours to come down from the 'high' of performing. His motoring habits made him uninsurable and he retired to the passenger seats of his Rolls Royce. The bike above is merely a prop to show off his then-favourite uniform - purchased, it is said, for $300 from a US policeman who was then left shivering in his bare essentials.

Above: Children of all ages at play outside the gates of Moon's Weybridge house.

'coming down' has always taken a lot longer. Especially for Keith and Peter. Keith would get into mischief because he couldn't just go to bed and stop, with all that adrenalin still running round his body.

My first personal experience of this was after a gig at Sussex University. We asked Keith back to the house, but with its dim lighting and not very loud music, we didn't offer him enough excitement. Just as his chauffeur, who was starving, was about to put his food into his mouth, Keith said: 'We're off.' And disappeared into the night in his lilac Rolls Royce.

The game that night was Aircraft Grounded By Fog. Keith, who could be most convincing when he was creating a role, marched into the foyer of a large hotel in Brighton and explained that all aircraft had been grounded by fog at Gatwick. He'd got 200 passengers grounded and he wanted to check them in for the night. He booked them all in, and then went round to another hotel and did the same thing there. So now he had 400 hotel rooms booked in Brighton. After that he went chasing police cars and asking the police, 'Do you know where I can get a spot of crumpet?' He was always very good at getting on with the police, at persuading them to help him out, regardless of what he said.

At about four o'clock his poor chauffeur staggered back. We gave him his food, then he had to be off again because Moon was already somewhere else. He was running mad, and just could not relax. Even in the last interview I did with him he still said, 'I'm like an express train. It just takes so long to come down after a gig, I can't even speak to anyone for about an hour.'

That's how he tried to explain why he used to do all the terrifying things he did. But if you saw him perform, you could begin to understand. No one could put on a performance like that and be untouched by what he'd done.

Being a performer also has its social limitations. When you've finished work, everything is closed, everyone's gone home. Mooney used to say, 'I always get in somewhere at some club, and then get barred for life from it.'

There are still stories being told about Moon which I've never heard before, and some of them are quite incredible. One of the most extraordinary, which he told me himself, happened in Hollywood. He'd been

Drumming and fooling - the two sometimes inseparable - and at the controls of a hovercraft/toy purchased in Los Angeles.

to a party, I think with Oliver Reed, and there was a bet that he couldn't break into Mick Jagger's room at the Beverly Wilshire. He found out that Mick was on something like the eleventh floor, and he had a security man guarding his door. This made him decide he couldn't break in by any conventional manner, so he'd go up the outside. Just the idea of doing it gives me vertigo, without even considering that it was night and that Mooney was probably out of his brain at the time.

Anyway, he climbed up, he counted the windows along and got into the room. And there were Mick and Bianca. Mick woke up and pulled a gun on him–apparently he used to keep a gun under his pillow. Moon, said, politely: 'Good evening.'

When he saw who it was, Mick said, 'God, Keith, don't do things like that. I could have killed you.'

So Moon replied, 'Ah, what great publicity that would have been–"Stone Kills Rival".'

Bianca was apparently furious with Mick for pulling the gun on Moon, and it ended up with Moon and Bianca going out dancing while Mick went back to sleep.

Mooney was quite casual about the climb. 'If I thought I was going to fall off the building, I'd have fallen off, but I never think like that. If someone tells me I can't do something, I'll go on and prove I can.'

He could be frightening at times. He could switch, and suddenly from being just boisterous-mad he could become really menacing. The darker side was kept away from most people, but he told me he did suffer from depression, and insecurity of the Are-these-people-around-me-just-because-I'm-Keith-Moon? variety. His blacker antics included leaving piranha fish in baths in hotels, and putting them down the loo. And he used to carry small charges of explosive around with him and fix them to hotel doors. He'd put a charge on every door along a corridor and set them to go off in the middle of the night. When the people ran out, he'd be there shouting, 'Earthquake. Earthquake.'

Not surprisingly, he was very into fireworks. The Who had a party at Moon's house to launch the *Who's Next* album, and Mooney organized a firework display for it.

The house itself, incidentally, or rather its predecessor, had a pretty fiery history too. It was on the site of an old monastery in St Anne's Hill, Weybridge, and had been bought by Peter Collinson, the film director. It was said that there was hidden treasure there during the old monastic days. Indeed, the pub at the end of the road is called The Golden Grove. But Peter Collinson blew up the house. He blew it up and filmed the explosion and then he built the ultra-modern-looking house that Moon eventually took over.

The *Who's Next* party was held mainly in the grounds. Mooney's *pièce de résistance* that night was his own firework display. There were some wonderful set-pieces that made up pictures, and he even had one of the Queen. We all ooh-ed and aah-ed at that, and then carried on drinking.

The music was, of course, so loud it could be heard all over Weybridge, Chertsey –Surrey almost. Naturally there were complaints. The police turned up. No problem to Moon. Inside the house, there he was saying, 'Another drink, Inspector?' He'd had so many experiences of policemen being called out to 'deal' with him that he knew perfectly how to draw the sting out of them.

Apart from the prearranged occasions, and the things he did coming down from his highs after a performance, Keith was a passionate practical joker. Most people have heard about him smashing televisions and throwing hotel rooms out of the window. Especially Holiday Inns, I think it may have been their uniformity that got to him. But he would do subtler things as well. He would unscrew all the screws in the furniture and leave it all standing perfectly still and upright for the next person to occupy the room. As soon as they went in and moved a chair, it fell to pieces. If they put something on the table, it would crash to the floor.

At one period he had a Rolls Royce Corniche with a loud-hailer on it. He used to drive along the sea front at resorts in the West Country calling: 'Do not panic. Do not panic. There is a freak wave expected any

Such beautiful beasts.

Overpage: Need we say more?

minute. Do not panic. Please leave the beach.' Once he'd got people running up to the back of the beach he'd say, 'Don't, repeat don't, forget your shoes.' And people would turn round and start running back.

He used to go into High Street furniture shops with a picnic hamper and sit at one of the dining tables in the window. He'd take out champagne and chicken legs and salad and conduct a picnic in the middle of the furniture. When the perplexed manager inevitably challenged him he'd say, 'I'm just trying out this table . . . I'm thinking of buying one and I wanted to see what it was like to eat at.'

Some of his jokes needed a stooge to help him pull them. Branches of Marks and Spencer were one of his favourite targets. He'd grab an assistant and say: 'I'd like to buy a pair of trousers. Very strong trousers.' When the assistant brought a pair he'd say, 'They are strong, are they? They've got to be strong, tough trousers.'

While the assistant was assuring him about their strength, the stooge would pass by and Moon would say, 'Excuse me, Sir, would you help me with a little test?' The stooge, asking what he was going to have to do, was told, 'You just hold this trouser leg.' Moon held the other leg, and they tugged until the trousers ripped in half.

As those hideous 'supervisor' bells were rung, and the manager arrived, Moon would say, 'Ah, yes, yes. I think they might do. Could you wrap them please. Separately.' When the parcels were ready, he gave one leg to the stooge and kept one for himself. Then they'd go out of the shop, and walk off in different directions; each with a leg.

Another of Moon's combination stunts required someone else to dress up as a vicar and stand at a crowded bus stop. Then he'd drive up in the car, jump out and mug the vicar, and pull him into the car and drive off. What I could never understand was that pulling off the stunt was enough. He had no desire to go back to the scene of the crime and check out the chaos he'd caused.

It was astonishing how long it took him to burn off his energy. When he was living hard, no one could keep up with him. Perhaps you could for a day, but at the end of that time he'd be exactly the same, or even worse. He was like an engine that just

steamed and steamed; the pressure building ever upwards.

You could see it in his playing. He didn't play like any other drummer, he played like three drummers. If there was a gap that he could fill, he'd be in. He was totally committed to giving a high-energy performance, and couldn't have done it any other way. Living was a continual do-or-die affair. Even the rest of the band didn't know what he would do next. How can you make predictions about someone who'd jump out of a hotel window several floors up?

John Entwistle told that story. The Who were in the States, and one day when it was time to leave their hotel, John said to Keith, 'We've all got to be down in the bar in two minutes, and then we've got to leave.'

Keith said, 'All right, all right. I'm not ready yet but I'll be there. I'll see you in a minute.'

So John Entwistle was walking down the stairs towards the bar, when through the window on the landing he saw this body shoot past him on the outside. Rocketing into the ground. He thought, this is it. He's dead. He's going to be dead this time. But Moon was in the bar before Entwistle. 'Where have you been, John? Have a drink?'

Even after he was dead there was a feeling that he could not be separated from The Who. There was a *Tommy* party to help publicize the stage version of the rock opera. Roger didn't go, but Pete and John were there, and we all felt that though Mooney was dead, he was very much there in spirit. The party was in a great cavernous disco in the Charing Cross Road. It had a central area for dancing with tables all round. Part of the cabaret was a Wild West character who used a lassoo and a large whip.

There was also a disc jockey who played music in between the various acts. When he wasn't working he stood behind a curtain on a small stage. Then the Westerner got to the part of his act where he looked into a mirror and tried to shoot three balloons hanging behind him. He hit the disc jockey instead. People were slow to realize what had happened. Moans became audible, and then the disc jockey collapsed behind his curtain.

There was pandemonium. Someone rushed backstage and knocked over some inflammable material which was to be used for a fire-eating act, and this fell on some snakes belonging to a snake charmer. So within a few moments there had been a shooting, a fire, and an unpleasant smell of burning snakes. It could only have happened at a Who party. The police arrived, demanding names and addresses, followed by the fire brigade.

After they had established that the fire wasn't serious, the firemen stayed on. I can remember grabbing one of them and saying, 'Come and have a dance. I've always fancied firemen.' He was very tiny for a fireman, and looked petrified. It was a very bizarre evening, and I felt that Moon was overseeing the whole affair and smiling his approval. The only thing that wasn't funny was the shooting of the disc jockey. He seemed quite badly hurt at the time. Not having heard anything to the contrary, I can only assume that he got better.

I saw Mooney the night before he died. It was at one of Paul McCartney's Buddy Holly parties, at the Peppermint Park. Moon was a bit quiet, but he was all right, nothing to give rise to concern. Next day we heard that he was dead.

I was in the office at Radio One. John Peel's producer, John Walters, who had produced some radio shows Keith had done, and was very close to him, said: 'There's been an unconfirmed report to the news room that Keith Moon is dead.' We hoped it was a joke. A call to The Who's publicist, Keith Altham, confirmed that it was *not* a joke. But although no one really expected Keith to make the three score years and ten, it was still a shock. Roger said that Keith's funeral was the worst day of his life. 'I suppose I was still hoping that the whole thing was another Mooney practical joke. I really half-expected him to leap out of the coffin and say: "Fooled you".'

One thing was odd about his death. Not the way he died, because there's not much doubt that he just got it wrong. He constantly overindulged in everything, taking handfuls of pills, miles over the top of the dose. Perhaps it was bound to happen eventually that he would take a fatal overdose. I certainly don't think he meant to kill himself, but the strange thing – to me – was that he had rung up about ten days before and asked me to write his life story.

He said, 'Now I want you to write it, and we'll call it *The Moon Papers*. I shall come down to Brighton 'cos there are some nice pubs there, and . . .'

I got very stern with him. 'OK, Keith, it would be great. But it'll take a lot of hard work. Are you serious about this?'

He assured me he was. Of course it never happened. In retrospect I have asked myself why he wanted to get it all down just at that particular time.

The wreath that Roger Daltrey gave him . . . in the shape of a TV set with a bottle of champagne stuck through the middle of it.

Each year the Radio One DJs were required to die a little in acts of absurd daring at assorted race tracks. But the *real* Fun Day was the year the Bay City Rollers dropped in on Mallory Park.

I wouldn't have thought that working in radio would necessitate being strapped into a souped-up Escort Mexico and finding oneself on the grid at Mallory Park race track waiting for the flag to go down. PETRIFIED. And this was supposed to be a FUN day. A Radio One Fun Day, a regular event during the summers of the past few years.

Basically the idea was for Radio One to invade an established race meeting and put on additional events, sponsor races, invite star guests and put out a live broadcast from the track. By 'trailing' the event for a week or two beforehand on a national radio network, we could be pretty sure that a five-figure crowd would turn up. 'A day out for all the family' was the usual slogan. Proceeds from the gate went to charity. It was like being part of a football team – everyone wore their standard-issue Radio One white T-shirt with the red and blue logo and custom-made white anoraks which are startling enough for the organizers to spot Tony Blackburn wearing one a mile off.

I don't know whose idea it was that there should be a DJs' motor race . . . but eventually there we were lined up on the grid. In order to be allowed on a recognized track, every driver must have taken part in official practice on the day of the race, and we had also been for lessons at the motor racing school at Brands Hatch.

First the instructor lets you drive around the track at your own speed, and gives you marks for proficiency, which is as unnerving as taking a driving test all over again. Removing one hand from the steering wheel is considered a very serious offence, with a heavy penalty. I am not by nature a particularly fast driver, but I don't doddle along either. However, when the instructor took me round Brands at *his* speed I just clung to the thought that he didn't want to die either.

'Right, your turn,' he said, and we changed seats.

Well, I'm sorry, but it was a reflex action to take my foot off the accelerator and reach for the brake when approaching Druids at a speed faster than I'd ever driven before.

'Take your foot off the brake,' the instructor shouted. I did, and it was . . . wonderful. I suddenly understood why these lunatics risk their lives trying to race faster on four wheels than anyone else. I'd had some experience of these 'speedsters' before, while making documentaries for Beeb television on motor and motor cycle racing. Racing drivers are required to have a particular temperament with a low emotional range and, naturally, an enduring level of concentration. I was intrigued to discover too that racing drivers are sex objects. One Grand Prix driver told me all the girls he made love to wanted him to keep his racing gear on throughout the encounter. A bit uncomfortable I would have thought, but then . . .

The drivers' groupies differ from Rock and Roll groupies in that to justify their existence in the pits they've got to be 'useful'. So they equip themselves with clip-boards and stop-watches and time the laps. These always glamorous-looking ladies also bedeck themselves with other apparently necessary paraphernalia of the motor-racing groupie. The 'shades' are parked on top of the head, the camera is slung round the neck,

Noel Edmonds - the ace in our Brands Hatch team.

the equivalent of the back-stage pass is clipped provocatively to the back pocket of the jeans. I've never seen such pre-meditated posing.

Well, *I* didn't feel anything like a sex object while sitting on the grid at Mallory Park. 'Don't take your foot off the clutch too quick or you'll stall,' warned a track marshal. We sat there revving–I'd never even driven in a car with a rev counter before–waiting for the flag. Once again it was prove-yourself time. Not only had I to 'drive' record programmes, now I'd got to prove myself with my male colleagues on a race track. That is, *I* thought I had to. The favourites that year were Rosko, Noel Edmonds, and, surprisingly, John Peel. I say surprisingly because such a mild-mannered man is actually a very zippy driver on the track.

We were off, and into the first right-hand bend. All my resolve to drive like the boys deserted me immediately. I slowed down–and was immediately overtaken by the entire field.

By the time I'd completed the necessary number of laps and got back to the pits it was a desolate area. Everyone, it appeared, had gone home. A certain eight-year-old who'd accompanied me to the track said: 'Oh God, how could you be LAST! What will I say at school tomorrow?'

Thus spurned I decided I must do better at subsequent Radio One Fun Days. At a Brands Hatch meeting it was decided that rather than risk our lives in a pukka motor race, we would go through the humiliation of a relay race. Two teams of DJs would have their members positioned round the track and each member would perform some risible feat to entertain the crowd which would also propel him/me further along the track. I got the kids's scooter. So did Paul Gambaccini, who was in the opposing team led by Rosko. Rosko's team were very keen on winning. In my team were Noel Edmonds, Simon Bates and Paul Burnett. The plan was that as we performed our various buffooning acts around the track, we would hand on the 'baton'–a plastic gold record–to the next person in the relay. Gambo and I waited in uneasy calm on the downhill stretch out of Druids Corner. Suddenly two cars came screeching round the bend. Which was my team's car? They looked exactly alike, and so did their helmeted drivers. Panic and much dodging to and fro took place. I grabbed my 'baton'. What to do with it? You can't 'scooter' all that successfully with a plastic gold record in your hand? I stuffed it down the front of my jeans. And scooted off. Paul was in the lead. I caught him up. Unbelievably I overtook him. I was very out of breath. A small crowd on that side of the track cheered. I completed my part of the course, handed over my baton and collapsed into the grass at the side of the track. I had to wait there until Head Driver Noel Edmonds came round the track again to collect me–the last one in the team. He would then drive us all back to the grandstand where we would leap out and then had to run 25 yards to the finishing line. The first whole team across the line would be the winners.

Before the race our team had a meeting to discuss tactics. 'Right,' I said to Noel. 'You'll be picking up Simon then Paul so they'll go into the back of the car, and I can leap into the front as the last member of the team you will pick up.' OK.

When Noel's car appeared again round Druids, the front passenger door swung open, arms reached forward, grabbed me and the car roared off again. To my horror I realized that the entire team was bundled into the two small front seats. Noel, an experienced racing driver, and therefore very fast, Paul, Simon (who is a well-built chap) and me. My head was rammed up against the roof of the car and my body pressed against the door. If the pressure of the four of us forces the door open I'll be first to roll out onto the track, I thought. And, at the speed we were travelling, to certain serious injury or death. I also knew that we were breaking all the rules of motor racing, i.e. that everyone MUST wear a safety harness and helmet while on the track.

Noel screeched to a stop, we tumbled out and staggered across the finishing line. Of course we'd saved valuable seconds by all travelling in the front of a two-door car, and we won. Afterwards Paul Gambaccini said to me: 'Gee, I was really worried, sitting in the back without a safety belt!'

On the last Fun Day at Brands Hatch, the Head of Games thought up an even better stunt. I discovered this information first as a Horrible Rumour. 'Have you heard? We're going to lie on the track and some stunt motor cyclist is going to jump over us?' No, I thought, Radio One wouldn't risk the lives of so many household names. As it turned out, they would. It got to be: 'Well, everyone else is going to do it, so you'll look a sissy if you chicken out.' Yet again one had to prove oneself One Of The Boys.

'Look there's absolutely NO risk,' they said. 'Would we endanger your lives? Of course not!'

The newspapers reported that we were being insured for a million pounds. I fell for it. When I saw the puny, trembling three-foot plank that Eddie Kidd the motorcyclist was going to use as his ramp to leap over 12 prostrated DJs, I have to admit I was, well, concerned. We all drew straws to decide who would be in the equivalent of the Hot Seat – the farthest away from the ramp. Tony Blackburn got it. That day he won my undying respect as the only one of us who

honestly appeared to be not in the least scared. The rest of us had spent the previous week working out trajectory angles and just what the degree of risk was.

We lay down in line on the track. I was No 5, sandwiched between Simon Bates and John Peel. The photographers moved in, and Eddie revved his engine. Only a week beforehand, another stunt motor-cyclist had died when he failed to clear a line of double-decker buses. The TV news pictures of that tragedy floated before my eyes.

Suddenly there was the roar of a motor-cycle engine past my ears, and a gasp from the crowd. Eddie had pretended he was going for the jump, then at the last second swerved past the ramp and driven within a hair's breadth of our unprotected bodies. *Très amusant.*

Then the two planks and metal frame which constituted the ramp were inspected one last time and Eddie prepared himself for the jump. Dave Lee Travis and Peely exchanged gags as we lay on the tarmac. Suppose, I thought, some pop music-hating, Radio One-loathing person had seen the jump as a glorious opportunity to wipe us all out in one fell swoop and bribed Eddie to 'pull' the jump . . . aargh. It was over in a matter of seconds and the picture of Eddie sailing over a row of disc jockeys made every national paper the next day.

A week or so later I mentioned to one of the Radio One organizers that I'd been relieved that at least we'd been insured for the sensible sum of a million quid.

'Insured? You must be joking. Who do you think would have insured you?'

Fortunately the Radio One Fun Days were varied in their DJ participation. Sometimes just to turn up, sign autographs, smile and wave was enough. This was my brief for another appearance at Mallory Park, which turned out to be the *real* fun day.

In 1975 Radio One invited the Bay City Rollers along as guests at a Fun Day at Mallory Park. The word Rollermania hadn't been invented. In fact 'mania' hadn't been justified as a suffix since the days of Beatlemania about 10 years before.

It only really began to dawn on us that the Rollers had turned into objects of mania while we were driving to Mallory Park. The traffic was immense, and the drive from a

Eddie Kidd, were it not for whose skill Radio One might have found itself advertising for 12 DJs.

friend's house which should have taken 20 minutes took about two and a half hours. As we crawled closer to the race track, we saw what looked like some Pictish invasion. Hordes of Rollermaniacs were coming over the hillside in their tartan scarves, short-sleeved shirts and cut-off trousers with tartan trim. They were the original Tartan Army (never mind Rod Stewart) but very mod-like with their luminous socks and spiky haircuts. It's strange the way these fashions interrelate: mod, skinhead, Roller, punk. Worse was to follow.

To make clear what happened next I should explain something of the layout at Mallory Park. Inside the race track is a lake,

and in the middle of the lake is a small island which the race people use for marshalling and as an observation point. Access to the island is via a wooden bridge. On this memorable day, the island was a BBC redoubt, with a hospitality marquee and a tower at the top of which David Hamilton (then a Radio One person) was doing his live bit, e.g. 'It's all going on here this afternoon, folks . . .' We stood there on this little island and looked across. We just could not *believe* the crowd, the thousands upon thousands of kids who had come to see the Bay City Rollers.

Once things started, I was out and about being one of the Fun Day people, which meant for example being trundled round the

track on the back of a trailer with the other DJs and doing a lot of waving. There was a Womble, too, who came with us, possibly it was Uncle Bulgaria. As if you care.

Back on the island helicopters were landing other guests—the Three Degrees and the like. By now the island was choc-a-bloc, and people were starting to overflow from the hospitality tent. Then the Rollers arrived. The pilot had a square of just a few feet in which to land the helicopter. As it came down, people were having to duck. Blades nearly whisking their hair off. Then all of a sudden there was a great roar from across the other side: 'AAAAAAAAAH!'

Thousands of young girls were running

Frenzy and distress at Mallory Park as Rollermania erupted among the tartan hordes.
Above: The Bay City Rollers leap from their temporary refuge in a boat onto the island, where a helicopter whisked them away to safety.

across the track—while there was a race going on. Having got across the track the girls were throwing themselves in the water to cross the lake to where the Rollers were. The basic fault was that no one had realized just how popular the Bay City Rollers had become, and therefore no one knew how to handle the situation. Least of all the police, who were busy grabbing girls and throwing them out of the lake, really chucking them on the ground.

A distraught - and dripping - Roller fan pleads in vain with an implacable crowd marshal (out of shot) to let her onto the island sanctuary from which her idols were trying to escape.
Opposite: My Old Man . . . otherwise Binky Baker, composer and singer, whose altercation at Mallory Park with 'the real Tony Blackburn' may or may not have inspired him to write the cult ditty Toe Knee Black Burn. Above his head, the four-badge set issued by Stiff Records who released this masterwork.

The Bay City Rollers were meant to do a lap of honour, but that was soon abandoned, and then the problem was how to get them away. They couldn't bring the helicopter back down to get the Rollers off because there were so many kids swarming all over the island. So they put them in a boat on the far side of the island. If anything, this was worse, because now the Rollers were marooned in the middle of the lake. Girls were wading in after them, grabbing the side of the boat. Tam Paton, their manager, didn't seem to mind. He was calculating, no doubt, the press coverage there would be if one of the band fell in the water. Suddenly Les McKeown was pushed over the side of the boat. Of course, the prospect of 'Roller Drowning!!' really got the girls going frantic. 'Les! Les!' they screamed, and hurled themselves back in the water again to get at him.

It was all beginning to get a bit intractable. But at least by that time the police had controlled the crowd. They'd had to stop the racing, because of the obvious danger of girl fans being mown down. The Rollers were removed from the lake and put in the tower.

So then there was a new ridiculous situation with the Bay City Rollers marooned in the tower, and the helicopter pilot not wanting to come down because of the great crowd still on the island. The organizers, in fact all of us, were really scared that someone would have their head removed by a rotor

of times Johnnie kept disappearing to go to the loo. At one point Johnnie Walker was talking to Tony Blackburn when Binky came past and said, 'Er, sorry. Your 15 minutes is up. You should go back to the loo now.'

Blackburn turned round and said, 'Do you mind! I'm trying to have a serious conversation.'

So Binky's reply to this was jovially to pour a port and brandy over Tony Blackburn's head. There followed one of those incidents which confirms my belief that Radio One is like being back at school. Blackburn of the Upper Fifth sneaked to Head of Games Johnny Beerling, the executive producer who was masterminding the afternoon, walkie-talkie and all, and complained.

'Please, Sir, will you tell her boyfriend not to pour drinks over me?'

And so Johnny Beerling came up to me and said, 'Would you please ask your boyfriend to desist from pouring drinks over Tony Blackburn?'

For months after that, people said to Binky, 'You did that? Cor! Can I buy you a drink?' and he basked in the role of The Man Who Poured Port And Brandy Over Tony Blackburn.

Years later, the name of the well-loved disc jockey must have been lurking somewhere in Binky's head when he was composing a new tune. He found himself using the words 'Tony Blackburn, Tony Blackburn' as a dummy lyric. Then he got to thinking it might do quite well as a real lyric. He changed it round a bit, and it eventually appeared in its final form as *Toe Knee Black Burn*. The record achieved cult status and might have climbed even higher than No 92 but for the fact that The Real Tony Blackburn, as he is known in our house, liked it. He kept playing it, which rather discouraged other disc jockeys of the Upper Remove from playing it whilst having a good snigger.

blade because the girls were still desperate to get to the Rollers. In the end the pilot got down after several attempts, the Rollers made a run for it from the tower, and escaped.

Once the Rollers had gone, the rest was mostly anti-climax. Except for an interesting little contretemps involving Binky and Tony Blackburn. Binky had been having a running gag with Johnnie Walker about the number

Wily members of the 'dole-queue generation' pull the plug on Rock's increasingly remote Superstars.

Street Credibility means, I suppose, not being a phoney, a poseur or a hypocrite. Not having too much money, not being flash and, more important, being able to relate to people *on* the street. It's part of the great British snobbery about success and making a fortune–which is still 'not done'. But, if such a misfortune should overcome you, you must at all costs keep quiet about it.

Rock stars began to blow their credibility when they fled Britain to tax havens. When they began to talk, like managing directors of record companies, of 'shifting units'–meaning selling records. When *they* became company directors, at least in the public eye, rather than musicians. The solid mass of Rod Stewart's Tartan Army–who would turn up at Faces concerts dressed like him, hair cut spiky like his and swaying together Cup Final-style with outstretched scarves–were entitled to feel bitter when he ponced off to Hollywood to live in a mansion with Peter Sellers's ex-wife.

The timing was so bad. In Britain it was the horrors of the three-day week, the energy crisis, the lack of petrol, and the now much publicized 'dole queue kids'. Many Punk bands were still on the dole after becoming nationally known figures. How could the jobless schoolleavers afford to come to Wembley and pay five quid a ticket to see Rod Stewart on perhaps his only visit to Britain that year? And while it might seem OK for the Bee Gees to turn to disco and count their money (and vulgar gold bracelets and medallions) in the sunshine of Florida, it didn't mean much to a kid from Deptford.

Characters from the Punk/New Wave revolution: Jimmy Pursey of Sham 69 and (opposite) Ian Dury, together with the cover of the album that sent Rock - and graphics - into a new era.

It was a miserable mid-decade. All the hope of the '60s with its affluence, its Carnaby Street and King's Road 'style' was now a shabby mockery. Those who'd got established in the late '60s – The Stones, Beatles, Twiggy, The Who, Small Faces, Kinks, David Bailey, Lichfield, Mary Quant, Deep Purple, etc., hung onto their crowns. Record companies invested more and more to promote their million sellers: Streisand, Paul Simon, the Moody Blues. Only the gentler forms of rock music – Genesis, Yes, Pink Floyd, Emerson, Lake and Palmer – were able to move with the others into the front line. Theirs was 'respectable' music – made for people, I've always suspected, who didn't like Rock and Roll in its raw form. The successful rock musicians grew older, richer and, many of them, fatter. They took their fans with them . . . but where was the music for the 15-year-olds? Were they to have to put up with The Wombles, The Osmonds, David Cassidy, The Jacksons? It was still the era of the singer-songwriter, mostly from the West Coast. Joni still ruled, so did James Taylor, Neil Young, Stephen Stills.

Bowie was the hope. And at the beginning of the decade the feeling was very much, in the media anyway, who is going to be The Beatles of the '70s? Because of the phenomenal success of the Fab Four in the '60s, it was naturally presumed that the whole process would be repeated again in the next few years. Radio One used to run a series called *The Sound Of The Seventies*. Actually it was the sound of the late Sixties, but one can only say that fairly with hindsight.

Maybe we were looking too hard. And trying too desperately to create a new phenomenon. Bowie held the front position for a few years. His fantasy figures, his startling 'look', plus his ability to envelop a unique futuristic image made him unsurpassed. But: WOULD HE BE AS BIG AS THE BEATLES? We wanted someone to put on a pedestal. As it happened, Bowie didn't have that kind of mass appeal, and perhaps never wanted it. He'd appear in an ever-changing procession of fantasy creations, and, I've often thought, lost his own identity in the process. But he was a fantastically influential figure.

'In 1976 you could *not* get a record deal if you were unknown,' said Sting some years later, who then was doing well to make a few quid a week as a semi-pro jazz band bass-player in Newcastle.

Something had to happen. In New York Malcolm McLaren tried it with the New York Dolls. It worked – a bit. He came back to London and formed the Sex Pistols with Rotten, Cook, Jones, Matlock and Vicious. That was the turning point. A generation found its identity. Disillusionment, anarchy – the New Wave. A revolt against glossy soulless professionalism, against rich Rock that spent hundreds of thousands of dollars in a recording studio, then passed on the costs through a gatefold album cover and expensive artwork. After the Sex Pistols *anyone* could get up and play. It didn't matter if you'd mastered your instruments. It didn't matter about record companies, and the huge advances they'd bestow on the lucky few.

The whole movement had to be built on adult-alienation – and that wasn't so easy. The adults had been brought up on images of drug abuse, sexual extravaganzas, Alice Cooper's horror shows. It was going to take a lot to shock 'em. Revulsion was the way.

'Johnny Rotten Never Cleans His Teeth,' said the papers. 'Young Punks Gob At Stage.' 'Punks Don't Like Sex.' Great stuff, so bewildering to the older generation. So were the torn T-shirts, sharp metal objects stuck through their noses and ears, bondage clothes, and incontinence 'nappies' slung behind their bums.

But if the Pistols were to have a movement, they needed followers to spread the word. Siouxsie saw the Pistols at The Screen On The Green. It affected her a lot. 'For the first time ever I felt part of what was going on.' McLaren offered Siouxsie a spot before the Pistols at the 100 Club. She had never been on a stage before, or written songs or sung or played an instrument.

'We got a sort of band together and Sid [Vicious] said he'd drum for us. We thought

Revulsion therapy was what Malcolm McLaren, the Svengali of Punk, decided the public needed – and he gave it to them through the Sex Pistols.
Overpage: New faces of Rock . . . Madness, Siouxsie, Blondie, Dury, Jam, Rotten – why, even Heartbreak Hotel came under new management.

THE JAM

we'd ruin something, like maybe a Bay City Rollers song. We called it *The Lord's Prayer*. It went on for half an hour. It was a mixture of nerves and excitement. We did what everyone was talking about–about not needing to know how to play guitar. Whereas bands like The Clash were musicians who'd been playing in small bands before. They were in a sect and we were the only ones who didn't belong to any of that.

'It annoyed a lot of people, that first time, but everyone was looking at us. It was really packed in there, sweat rising up from the bodies. No gobbing, that came with the labelling, when Punk became a fashion-fad . . . But even when we were quite a well-known name we were still on the dole, we didn't have a record deal, and we didn't have any equipment except for the guitars and drum sticks. We had to turn up and say to the other band, "Oh, our van broke down with all our equipment and we've hitchhiked all the way to the gig. Can we borrow your gear?" It became quite an art. Some of them got a bit stroppy, but they always lent us their gear. And now we've got a record deal, we've got our own equipment but we're borrowing other bands' musicians.'

Because of my 'Establishment' connections with the *Daily Express,* I thought it pointless to try to contact Rotten at the height of the Sex Pistols' infamy. They were tetchy days for the media who really were shocked and horrified by the behaviour of those 'appalling' people. Which meant they got more coverage. Malcolm's plan was

working . . . I bumped into Bill Grundy the day after his dreadful TV confrontation with the Pistols and teased him about it. The pompous broadcaster was not amused. If he had dared these young desperados to swear on live television, did he not really expect them to live up to their reputation?

The media reaction to the Pistols amused me greatly because they all pretended it had never happened before. But you could have swapped Sex Pistols' headlines for those put up on Rolling Stones' news stories ten years or so before. 'Pop Star In Drug Overdose Mystery', 'Pop Star Girl Friend: Drug Probe', 'Police Probe Pop Star Drug Death' . . . no permutation went unexplored.

The only difference seemed to be that neither Rotten nor Vicious was projected as a sex symbol in the way Jagger had been (though, incidentally, I had dozens of letters from girls begging me to put them in touch with Rotten).

Finally when I met Rotten he was complaining about police harassment, dawn raids *à la* 'Police Swoop In Dawn Raid on Pop Star', about having his door broken down while he was put on charges of possessing offensive weapons. Almost word for word it was the same experience that John Lennon went through when he became the prime prey for ambitious Drugs Squad ferrets.

The hard-core Punks with their nihilistic attitude kicked open the door for the opportunists. I honestly believe that the first wave of successful bands was made up of reasonably competent musicians who

pretended they couldn't play for the sake of fashionable credibility. The Clash had always been able to play. The Buzzcocks were a pop band with a built-in writer in Pete Shelley, who amid the images of violence remained one of the gentlest people I've come across. And how was it that the evil-looking Stranglers, having established first base with a hit record, suddenly sounded like The Doors and just as polished?

Only Bob Geldof of the Rats was honest enough to admit: 'I'm in this to get rich, get famous and get laid.' All of which he's managed to achieve–plus writing the classic *I Don't Like Mondays.*

Within a year and a half the so-called 'progressive new wave' was beginning, to me anyway, to sound suspiciously like pop music. But what the hell, it's some of the best pop music Britain has ever heard. And after the stultifying boredom of the early '70s it was a blast of fresh air. It happened through necessity and enterprise. Although the major record companies opened their double doors and signed up repugnant, to them, Punk bands they then had the problem of sorting out the best from the riff-raff.

The open doors and open cheque books slammed shut again. Those that were already through–The Rats, XTC, Clash, Stranglers were safely on the circuit. The rest decided to make their own records. Small labels were set up–Factory, Deptford Fun City, which launched The Police and Squeeze–and of course Stiff. (A 'stiff' in record company parlance means a flop. So it was cocking a snook from the start.)

The new music was great if you couldn't dance, or just hated Disco. Anyone could pogo - and if you were at the back it was a good way of glimpsing the band. Then Chas Smash of Madness took it all 'One Step Beyond'.

Stiff was started by Dave Robinson and Jake Rivièra for a reputed £200. They thought up a clever marketing idea. Put out a record, sell as many as possible quickly, then delete it. Working on this short shelf-life theory they soon established the collectors-item syndrome. They also put out good records. The Damned's *New Rose,* and the songs of Elvis Costello and Ian Dury. A young chap calling himself Wreckless Eric sent in a tape to Stiff, who were operating from an estate agent's shop near Warwick Road tube station. Nick Lowe, the in-house producer, heard the tape, called Wreckless Eric in and recorded with him *Whole Wide World,* still one of Stiff's best.

Ian Dury's experience had been somewhat different. He was a lot older, a veteran of the London pub rock circuit. He'd made records before with Kilburn and the High Roads. The first record he made for Stiff—*Sex And Drugs And Rock And Roll*—was, I thought, intriguing. His appearance on the first Stiff tour convinced me that this diminutive figure with the gruff voice was a

performer of unique talent. It was Music Hall and Rock and Roll and charisma. The band weren't half bad either. Elvis and Wreckless and Nick Lowe and Larry Wallis were on the same tour. After the show Ian introduced me to Eric's parents: 'This is Wreckless Dorothy and Wreckless Frank.'

With the release of Ian's album, *New Boots and Panties,* not only Ian, but Stiff also, were on their way. They marketed their own image as much as their artists'. I became a fan of a record company! Their badges were masterly. Even these were 'limited editions'—perhaps a whole set to promote one single. You wore them at your peril. People would plead, and whine for the blue-background 'Sex And Drugs And Rock And Roll and Ian Dury' one. Their T-shirts as well were 'different'. The classic one said, in bold black letters: 'If it ain't Stiff, it ain't worth a fuck.' Their design department created crazy record labels, with lettering so small it was almost impossible to read. Or there would be no writing at all. This meant a little more care and attention for DJs

WRECKLESS ERIC....

NEW DOUBLE ALBUM OUT NOW FIRST 10,000 ONLY £3.99 (SEEZ 21)

SMA

BE·STIFF

REST

VENUE:

DATE:

wishing to play the record.

Bernie Andrews at the Beeb particularly objected to the label of Humphrey Ocean's Stiff single *Whoops A Daisy*. It's one of Bernie's idiosyncracies to object to obscure

The poster for a Wreckless Eric album, opposite, was typical Stiff bezazz, with special offer for the first 10,000 and other tricky inserts. Stiff kept up the onslaught with a steady spray of collectables, from passes to limited-edition badges and records that were rapidly deleted.

label designs. I called Stiff. 'Bernie won't let me play Humphrey's record because he can't read the label.' 'OK,' said Stiff. 'Can you get hold of a photograph of Bernie Andrews?' I could. Two days later a new copy of Humphrey's record arrived on Bernie's desk. It had a specially designed label, featuring Bernie's face, and clearly indicated the A and B side. We played the record. Of course this could be dismissed as grovelling to BBC producers, but I think it was more Stiff élan than anything else.

What was important about Punk was its originality. It was a means of expression that fitted the times. It must have hit the jeans empire for six, and killed the fashion garment business. Punks *never* wear jeans or expensive-looking clothes. Old clothes, too-large clothes were 'in'. Which was most convenient on the pocket. This was also born of necessity since Punks didn't have money. Or were not *supposed* to have. Girl Punks were gloriously vulgar and started wearing mini-skirts with suspenders. Their make-up was, of course, ghoulish. White face, eyes totally surrounded with black, black nails, black lips. And the HAIR. Hair was cut very short, girls and boys. It had to be dyed. Most popular colour first of all was Bowie red (his influence hadn't waned). Then there

was jet-black. Later came the colours. Purple, green, yellow, pink. A boy assistant at Smile, the hair chaps in Knightsbridge, dyed his hair white, and then added black musical notes into it. The effect was marvellous.

Punks started to influence graphics. The cut-out 'blackmail' lettering started by the Pistols changed the 'look' of music papers and magazines—first of *New Musical Express*—then spread to far more 'respectable' publications. Another influence was the Xerox style started by the fanzines.

A totally innovative factor of the Punk movement was that kids who wanted to communicate their own experiences other than through music, typed out their words on an office typewriter—or wrote them by hand—and sneaked into the photocopying room after hours to make copies. One secret missive read: 'I may have to stop in a minute . . . I'm not supposed to be in this office and I might get caught any second.' It communicated *perfectly*.

Film and television too was caught up with Punk. Even TV commercials—especially for fashion, cosmetics and sunglasses—now have that stark, fast-cutting shot-to-shot 'Punk' look. The fact that Malcolm McLaren should have insisted that the whole movement was masterminded by him as *The Great Rock and Roll Swindle* makes the final, fitting, perfect, twist.

Above: The amazing dress-style of Lene Lovich, layer on layer of lace, braids, plaits and ribbons in ways they'd never been seen before . . . not to mention the chilling hiccupy voice that seemed to come from over the graveyard wall.

Left: Some of the New Wave record sleeves that made sure you never knew what to expect.

Overpage: More memorabilia from an amazing period that began with The Beatles together and finished with the Sex Pistols disintegrating.

is
Up Escalator
RadioStars
BED PEACE
'John and Yoko'
THE RUM
FROGS SPROUTS CLOGS

LOVICH
ELECTR
ORCHES
ence
IN ASSOCIATI
TH
GRE
ROCK
RO
SWIN
WITH MUSIC BY
Sex Pist
UR
RAUTS

Tracking The Police through Tokyo, Hong Kong, Bombay and . . . Newcastle.

My relationship with The Police has been incident-prone from the very beginning. I am wondering if any reputable insurance company would contemplate an all-risks policy applicable to any confrontations therein and thereinafter to be known as a meeting, hereinafter to be designated as any occasion whereby the Insured is within fifteen feet of Sumner, Summers and Copeland.

Or maybe I bring *them* into potentially dangerous situations. In October '78 they came to Manchester to perform on *Whistle Test*. For them it was a major breakthrough. Radio One's vital playlist had not shared my enthusiasm for *Roxanne,* the first potential hit for The Police, because it was about a prostitute. Nor had they gone much on the follow-up, *Can't Stand Losing You,* as the picture bag wrapper showed a bloke hanging himself. I liked it even more than *Roxanne!* Only after *Roxanne* was a hit in America did Britain wake up to the talent of the band. And it's worth mentioning that The Police made the American hit by hopping on Laker to NY with one roadie carrying their equipment as hand luggage and playing for a hundred dollars or less a night to maybe 25 people. But they were 25 disc jockeys, radio station programme directors and journalists . . .

Back in Britain The Police now had the crucial task of breaking their first album, *Outlandos D'Amour.* Whatever the criticisms of *Old Grey Whistle Test* may be, it is acknowledged that almost any band who has the opportunity to play three live tracks from their new album on this the only rock show on British TV is going to jump at the chance.

Sting was also filming *Quadrophenia* at that time and had to be helicoptered after the show to Brighton for some beach scenes with Mods. The make-up room in the BBC TV studios in Manchester is more friendly than most, sort of a nice place to hang out if you want your hair bleached, your clothes

Below: On the seafront at Brighton for Quadrophenia, with Sting, centre, elegant in a grey silk suit.
Right: the debut album, Outlandos d'Amour.

Early publicity shots.

washed, eyebrows plucked or buttons sewn on. Sting walked in, and perceived a make-up lady struggling with an aerosol can, containing silver hair spray. 'Let me help you with that,' he said gallantly–and the can exploded in his face. Barely an hour before we recorded the show he was receiving treatment at Manchester Infirmary–a gloomy hospital I might say. There was no permanent damage to his eyes but nevertheless our first interview on TV was conducted with him wearing dark glasses over smarting eyes. It's not the easiest thing to play bass wearing too-large borrowed glasses sliding down your nose. 'And it was my birthday,' he recalled miserably.

We met again a few days later in Brighton where the director of *Quadrophenia,* Franc Roddam, had taken over the town with the help of 300 or so extras culled from Barnsley 5.15 Motor Scooter Club and the like.

The obliging Roger Daltrey, as an executive producer of the film, was busy signing autographs and saying to me: 'Go on, Annie, interview these guys–they're the *real* story.' Which meant I dutifully had to write down the names, ages, and occupations of 48 Mods, and had to take particulars of their scooters. Sting wasn't really a star then. But he looked outstanding with his 500-quid grey silk Mod suit among the warring factions of Mod extras, police extras and Rocker extras.

The staged battles on the beach were so authentically re-enacted that one Mod extra punched in the face of not a police extra, but a real policeman. Charges were not preferred. It was a jostling mass, and Mr Roddam confessed that he had pushed his luck in Brighton considerably during the location scenes to get what he wanted.

Well, anyway. Next time I met The Police was entirely by accident, in a room over a pub near Baker Street around Christmas '79, where they were being presented with various gold . . . platinum . . . plutonium albums. Through a chaotic number of misunderstandings, I found myself face-to-face not so much with them but with a movie camera and microphone.

Little did I then know their deep Desire To Document. Wisely or not, The Police film, photograph and record everything that happens to them . . .

I spent Christmas '79 innocently dancing at parties to the sound of *Message In A Bottle* and *Walking On The Moon.* Good pop group, yeah.

During the New Year *Mailbag* programme the Daily Mail astrologer predicted 'much travel in February and March' for me. Nonsense, impossible, I had thought, then two months later I was at the end of a 19-hour flight to Tokyo, about to start filming The Police's World Tour for an *Old Grey Whistle Test Special.* The band had by then been in Tokyo for two days and not wasted a moment equipping themselves with more documentary instruments–i.e. Nikon F2s, FEs, F1s, wide angles, star filters . . . you name it, they'd bought it. So I was greeted by click-whirr-click and the expensive whine of motor-driven cameras. I had fallen asleep during the drive from Narita Airport, only waking somewhat amazed at the under- and over-passes in Central Tokyo and wondering what alibi I could use to avoid going to their gig. To sleep, perchance–no chance. But as anyone knows who has had to override the body clock and carry on when every atom is screaming 'I want to go to sleep', it's very difficult then to sleep at all.

I refuse to believe in jet-lag–it's an attitude of mind. If you pick up on local time on arrival and assume it as normal–even though it's eight in the morning and you've got to carry on for another 12 hours–you can get by. Whereas people who keep telling you what time it is at home are doomed to suffer jet-lag.

Next day we left for Nagoya on the bullet train. The well-informed were at Tokyo Station to give the band a send-off. They had booked reserved compartments, followed the band off the train again at Nagoya and booked into the same hotel. They deluged the group with gifts. Stewart's favourite was a musical calculator. But they were all given flowers, chocolates, kimonos and letters like the ones reproduced on the next two pages–extraordinary for their gentle naivety, and poetry too, e.g. 'And did my sweat with deep inspiration reach you?' Come to think of it, the English is pretty good. (How would your average British fan make out in Japanese?)

Sanae
1-16-3 Itabashi
Itabashi - ku. Tokyo 173
JAPAN.

Mr. Sting
Police

Dear Sting

How do you do !
My name is Sanae - Utsushikawa.
I'm 17. and in 11th grade. of course
I'm Japanese.
I'm a big fan of Police. (especially yours!
You are crazy about playing roller - skate.
   aren't you?
I'm crazy about it too.
Right now. I'm playing roller skate very ha

    X   X   X
I was very very shocked when I heared
"Roxanne" for the first time!!
It is a sensational happening
          since then The Beatles!

DO SPORTS, DO STUDY, DO LOVE FOR THE FITNESS... A DO-GIRL IS NOW MOST FANTASTIC.

FLYING TIME
DJ38EE
No. 1110-W

I like also The Beatles.
But, now I like The Police best of all !
    and I love you.

I'm looking foward to buying all your new
records, so please keep well, and keep
on singing for a long time.
When at your leisure. call me Tel 964-4310
(It's a Joke ... ?)
Please say hello to your wife and son for me.
I will be a big fan of Police forever.

    With love
    Good-Bye.   Sanae.

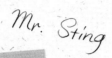

Mr. Sting

Seiko Ashiba

Sting,

am a Japanese girl of seventeen.
are a English man of twenty-six.
t you crossed the frontier into my heart.
give some power to every generation.

went to the concert of the Police last night.
could not sit still.
hat a wonderful space it was!
hy do you have such a strong power?
er you aware that your power lead me to have
a great power of my own?

I went to many rock concerts, but I didn't experience
shuch a concert as the Police.
It's not only full of vitality, but
also very beautiful.
I guess that beautiful feeling
which was the inside of your heart
appeared.
That superlative spirit which was
the sweat of your body sent out
to me.

And did my sweat with deep inspiration reach you?

I am so happy that there is such a man as you
and there is the Police in this world.
I can not write my thought well.
At any rate, you are a great important and
the most wonderful man in my life.

I can say the Police is the No.1 all over the world
and you too.
There is a lot of things in my head, but I am so deeply
moved that I cannot find out words.
I am crazy on the sounds of the Police.
I never forget a pleasantness that you gave me.
I guess I will close and I hope you send me
a message in the bottle.

With love from,
Seiko Ashiba
1-16-6 Zoshigaya, Toshima-ku,
Tokyo, Japan 171

17

The first night star
will bring you happiness

AI'SUKINA STING ᴴᴱ

Dear Sting
スティング!!

First and second concert
were very very good and excited!

But once they'd made their formal presentation, bowed and giggled behind their hands, that was it. They'd move off.

Japanese culture has been overwhelmingly influenced by the West and, among the young, chiefly by British pop music – curiously Japanese teenagers care more about what happens in Coventry and Manchester than in the geographically much closer Los Angeles. The Two-Tone cult had reached Japan when we arrived. In discos, at venues where The Police played the 'look' was black and white, copied from photographs of groups like The Specials and The Beat. One Japanese boy in a black shiny pork-pie hat tapped me on the shoulder and announced proudly: 'I am a Mod.' Yet he could have had no idea what 'Modernism', which began in the '60s in London and places like Brighton, was about. The sole points of reference for the Japanese are their

dozen or so glossy pop magazines such as *Music Life* whose pages are crammed with pictures and features about British rock stars.

It is the magazines here rather than records and radio which have caused this extraordinary fascination. Meeting Japanese pop fans also established a long-held theory of mine. Without intending any bigotry here, a race such as the Japanese has always appeared to me to be physically alike. I had often wondered whether we Europeans all looked the same to them. Sure enough I was told by many Japanese – You look like Suzi Quatro. Others drew my likeness with Bonnie Tyler . . . and others thought I was Sonja Kristina, Stewart Copeland's singer girlfriend! None of whom I look like.

Nagoya didn't look particularly Japanese. It's a business town, headquarters of Yamaha. And there at the gig, the Kinro Kaikan Hall, was the man who'd made it all

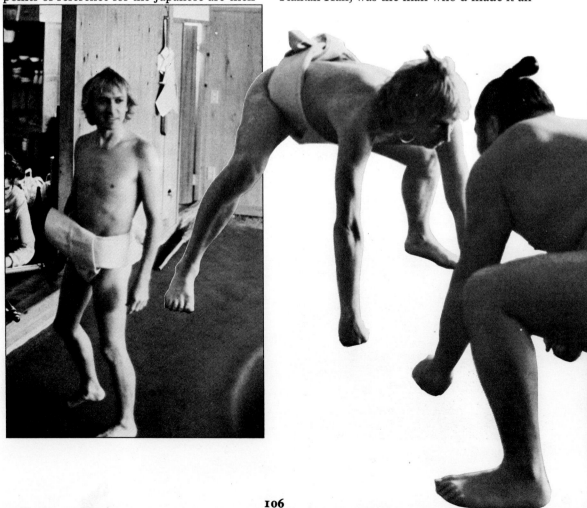

possible, Mr Udo, Japan's major promoter. Udo has brought to Japan most of the major rock acts . . . 'Eric Crapton (*sic*), Ten Rears After and the biggest of them all, Red Zepperin.' He was still trying to get over the Wings fiasco, and recover from the shock of being $2 million down when McCartney was imprisoned and had to cancel the tour, though Paul did see him alright later. Udo explained that he'd spent the past six years convincing the Minister of Justice that McCartney had now grown up and didn't take drugs any more. When the grass was found in McCartney's suitcase the Japanese customs arrested him but Udo said the authorities were very embarrassed at having such a celebrity behind their bars and they really didn't know what to do with him. 'Much loss of face for me,' said Udo. 'Much loss of face for Minister of Justice.'

Having been infiltrated by so many Western influences, the conservative Japanese government is determined that its young should not share in Western drug culture and its attendant problems. Possibly due to its proximity with South-East Asian drug-producing countries, the laws in Japan are stringent, harsh and effective. The Maclean modelling twins, Jenny and Sue, who were working in Tokyo while I was there, told me of an Australian model girl who was hounded out of Japan after she had given one spliff to a Japanese boy. Whereas later in India I was offered acid on the street, there was no evidence whatsoever of drug-taking by the Japanese.

A stern test for Andy when he demonstrated his enthusiasm for the martial arts. Eager promoters fixed up an encounter with a 20-stone Sumo giant. Andy bravely put on the ritual gear, mutual salutes were grunted and they met in earnest for a mercifully brief bout.

From Nagoya to Osaka we travelled on to Kyoto which really looks like everyone's concept of Japan. Snow-topped mountains and Buddhist temples. Each temple is framed by a Shinto gateway, and each one I found an awe-inspiring image. The temple area was some distance from the hotel and we were somewhat surprised to find that we were being followed by fans in taxis. It transpired that one particularly determined young lady had decided to cover the whole tour. Her parents had given her £400 to do so.

'Do they know what you're doing?' I asked her.

'Well I said I was going on a sight-seeing tour.'

Her name was Seiko and when we turned the cameras on her, we were politely stopped by the record company representatives. 'Don't film her,' they said, 'she's the Shame of Japan.' All the more reason to film her.

Japan's prosperity obviously has come about through the success of its multinational companies. Young people are under pressure from an early age to find a reasonable position in a reputable company and are then expected to stay with the company for the rest of their lives. Changing jobs is somewhat frowned on. After all the company takes you into its 'family', paying for holidays and weddings. The pressure on young people to 'get on' is far greater in Japan than Britain. Parents, though, will treat their children to a 'binge' now and then, which not infrequently allows for a pop fan to follow his or her heroes around the country as Seiko did. Whether Japanese parents realize that this could cause moral decline in their young, I did not discover!

Hong Kong was as breathtakingly spectacular as it was a beautiful surprise. The Pan-Am Jumbo dived in out of the sky, swooping low over the harbour dazzling with lights and reflections of floating restaurants.

In Hong Kong I would have something to do at last. Which was to present The Police with two British Rock and Pop Awards. These awards are organized jointly by BBC *Nationwide,* Radio One and the *Daily Mirror.* The previous year at the first presentation, all the artists who'd won, or most of them, were at the Cafe Royal in London to collect their awards. On this occasion hardly any winners were in Britain. There was no way The Police could fly back to collect their awards—for Best British Group and Best Album. (Incidentally they either won or came second in every possible category.) Nor could Gary Numan fly back from America to collect the Best Male Singer award nor Jerry Dammers of The Specials—also in America—to collect the DJs' award, nor Cliff Richard from South Africa.

Nationwide therefore decided to link up by satellite to the various parts of the world where the winners were. And if necessary fly 'celebrities' out to make the presentation. A costly business in view of the much publicized cut-backs at the Beeb. As I was going to be with The Police in Hong Kong, I was 'offered' as a hander-over of the prizes. I think *Nationwide* initially wanted someone more prestigious . . . like Andy Gibb, who after all was, as *Nationwide* put it, 'brother of the previous year's winners, the Bee Gees, AND a world recording star in his own right.' Well in the end he didn't get the gig. He was persuaded to open an important envelope in London. Back in Hong Kong I was to make the presentation during a special satellite link which would be shown on a large screen back at the star-studded Cafe Royal presentation lunch. Because of the time difference—eight hours—The Police would be on-stage when *Nationwide* required them. The gig was a plush place called, Today's World Disco, all blue perspex and chrome, and the satellite coverage was to be done by Hong Kong TV. There appeared to be no problems. At the appropriate moment I would leap on-stage, stop the music and hand over the first award—Best Album of '79, *Reggatta de Blanc*—to Sting.

Rehearsals in the empty disco during the sound-check in the afternoon revealed no hazards. The Police were to do a split set of 45 minutes each, the first to coincide with the satellite link-up. Various signals were agreed and theoretically I should leap on the stage as they played *Walking On The Moon.* A Chinese floor manager was to tap me on the back as a cue when he got word from London

Hong Kong poster - and true British disgruntlement in one of several letters written to the Press.

THE POLICE

On 26th & 27th February

At Today's World Disco

今日世界

TODAY'S WORLD DISCO

440 Jaffe Road 1/F Lockhart Bldg., Wa...

Lee Gardens Hotel. Hysan Avenue, Hong Kong. Telephone: 5-767211. Cable Address: LEEGARDENS.

Lee Gardens Hotel HONG KONG

Next To You
So Lonely.
Death Wish
FALL OvT
Hole in My LIFE
TRUTH HITS

WALKing on the Moon

By the time we arrived back in the evening the audience were in, and tightly packed around the stage. The Chinese floor manager was trying to hear his instructions from the Outside Broadcast Scanner (mobile studio) parked down in the street. From there would come the instructions from London. Unfortunately he couldn't hear. Anything. The whole operation required, I had been told, split-second timing, otherwise we would lose the satellite. I waited, being jostled and pushed by the dancing, bopping audience for the tap on the back. The Chinese floor manager, bent double out of camera range, held the headphones tighter and tighter to his ears. All one could hear was a high-pitched whine and a gabble of Chinese. The time to leap on the stage came. No tap on back. The band, as agreed, played *Walking On The Moon*. Sting made it local and sang 'Walking in Kowloon'. The band played on. And on. The longest version of the song they'd ever done. But there was no way of telling the band that something had gone wrong. Eventually they exhausted all possible variations and came off-stage.

'Where the hell were you Annie?' shouted a bewildered Stewart.

We all retired to the dressing-room.

'No. No you back on stage. Now,' shouted the agitated Chinese floor manager.

'No, we won't', said the band. 'We've finished for now.'

No one wanted to fake the presentation. The Chinese floor manager told the Scanner to tell London that we weren't going back on stage. In rather the manner of a Judy Garland-Micky Rooney movie we hit on an idea. 'Let's do it right here—in the dressing-room. It'll look more natural.' This was agreed, but we still had no idea when and if The Word from London would come. We might get only a few seconds' warning. Or more. Or not. We waited. We decided that the camera should be positioned inside the dressing-room door and that at the given moment—if it ever came—I should burst through, and 'surprise' the band. My cue this time was to be a tap on the leg from the Chinese floor manager.

Running order for the Hong Kong fiasco which included a unique half-hour rendition of Walking in Kowloon.

OK. Right. This was it. We were ready. Poised. Oh God, no one's miked up! I suddenly realized. A lot of good *silent* presentations would be! That problem was solved and we waited. The Chinese floor manager, still frowning, perplexed, into his headphones, became more and more agitated. He crouched under the camera, poised for The Moment. In his agitation he grabbed my right leg—'Great, at last the cue.'

'No, no, not yet.'

'But I thought that was the cue.'

'No, no, not yet.'

In his nervousness tapping me on the leg had become a compulsive twitch. Then at last, progress. 'Three minutes from now.' OK. We counted down. Two minutes . . . one minute . . . thirty seconds . . . then he'd shake his head.

'Not yet. Aye minute.'

OK. Eight minutes. Seven. Six. Five. No, no' yet. Start again. I maintained what I call ICY CALM in these situations, but I was beginning to wonder what Sting, Andy and Stewart, plus the fun-loving film crew would be getting up to behind the closed door, where they were even less informed about what was going on than I was. I envisaged that when I finally did burst through the door they would be stark naked— or worse, not there at all. Having climbed out of the window. I had been told over and over by *Nationwide* that there would be one and a half minutes, and one and a half minutes ONLY for me to present the award, and hand back to the Café Royal.

After at least half a dozen false grab-me-by-the-legs, it appeared we were in a go-situation. I burst through the door clutching the damned award under my arm, and Andy exclaimed:

'It's Eamonn Andrews!'

It was a bit like *These Are Your Lives*. Trying to appear unperturbed, I turned to Sting and said, 'Well, when you made *Reggatta de Blanc* did you ever imagine you'd be collecting an award for it in Hong Kong?'

'Yes,' said Sting, deadpan.

This got a huge laugh at the Café Royal. The reasons were both obvious and complex. The audience back in London were by now in a state of hysteria. Right from the start the Rock and Pop Awards had been a fiasco.

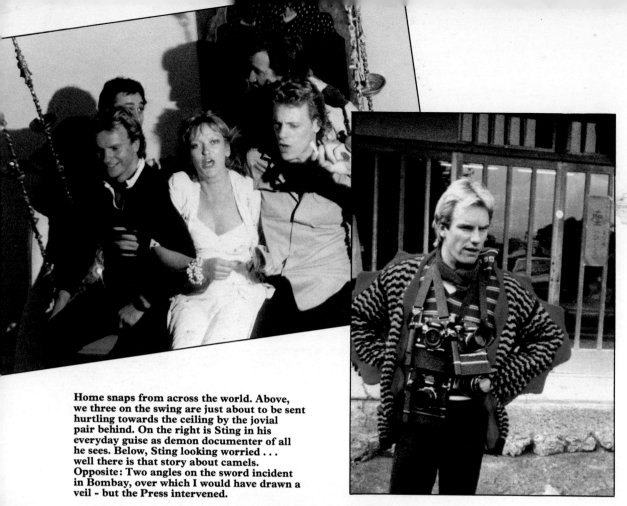

Home snaps from across the world. Above, we three on the swing are just about to be sent hurtling towards the ceiling by the jovial pair behind. On the right is Sting in his everyday guise as demon documenter of all he sees. Below, Sting looking worried . . . well there is that story about camels. Opposite: Two angles on the sword incident in Bombay, over which I would have drawn a veil - but the Press intervened.

EMPIRE DAYS

THE RAJ has left its mark most obviously in the form of red double decker buses, driving on the left, cricket matches and a quite disarming olde English courtesy everywhere.

☐ YOU need to go out in the early hours to witness Bombay's most appalling spectacle—hundreds of thousands of people from tiny babies to old men, sleeping out on pavements and window ledges all over the city. I even spotted several men who were sleeping out stark naked.

☆ Everyone knows cows are sacred in India. But did you know they actually keep these beasts tethered inside their temples?

A messy business.

☐ Police have made such an impact on Bombay that they are already drawing up plans for a return concert next year. No doubt other bands will follow through the door they have opened.

TOP TEN SINGLES

1 Going Underground — The Jam. 2 Turning Japanese—The Vapours. 3 Dance Yourself Dizzy—Liquid Gold. 4 Together We Are Beautiful — Fern Kinney. 5 Working

Ad Lib

From JOHN BLAKE in Bombay with Police

Annie got stung when she crossed swords with Sting

I'VE HEARD of ladies defending their honour, but I fear Annie Nightingale, Old Grey Whistle Test's husky voiced presenter, took the whole concept too far this week.

The delectable Miss Nightingale, who is making a BBC documentary about Police's world tour, challenged overtired and emotional lead singer Sting to an early morning sabre duel in a suite at the plush Taj Mahal Hotel

Sparks flew as the pair lunged and parried with swords borrowed from a photo session, while I discreetly dived underneath a coffee table.

The unseemly fracas ended only when Sting unchivalrously attempted to chop off Miss Nightingale's finger, thus spilling precious drops of her blood onto the rug.

Fortunately the monstrous Sting had sufficient decency to stick an Elastoplast on her battle wound before grovelling his apologies.

I think they are still friends.

Annie and Sting: duel

He's sewn up a fort

IF YOU bought the shirt or jacket you are wear a trendy London boutique, there is more tha chance that your garment was stitched togethe steamy heat of this insane city.

Take Six, for example, buy vast quantities of clot a Bombay company run by a charming gentlema Parsu Amersey. By a string of coincidences I found invited to lunch with Mr. Amersey at his vast air-con white mansion in Bombay's leafiest suburb.

Mr. Amersey told me that he needs to employ 16 a in order to run his home properly. Of course, I said thing else he said was quite interesting: The 1,800 who stitch together his clothes for Take Six and London boutiques earn, on average, £10 a week.

Snakes alive— what a charmer

IF YOU THINK the busker with the budgies in Leicester Square is spectacular, you wouldn't believe this place.

At well as fire eaters and snake charmers, I've also spotted a chap who was staging pavement fights to the death between mongooses and cobras—at £5 a time.

As far as i could tell the mongooses always won.

☐ THEY don't curries here like th in Finchley Road. Most of them vegetarian for a star the speciality being thing called a thali consists of lots of dishes of spicy vegetables and you served up with puff on a silver tray. Oh McDonalds!

☐ I WOULDN'T complain that its too hot here, but—with temperatures in excess of 120 degrees, I really did see for the first time the legendary spectacle of a man frying an egg on the pavement.

GIGS TONIGHT

The TV presentation was supposed to start with a group of girls dancing to a medley of songs by winning artists. For heightened effect dry ice was pumped onto the vinyl stage. There are two types of dry ice, water-based and oil-based. Oil-based dry ice was used on this occasion. It evaporated onto the vinyl floor. Consequently the dancers came on–and promptly fell over. They started the show again–it was being recorded for transmission the following day. The dancers fell over again. And again. SEVEN times.

The last I saw of The Police in Hong Kong was them disappearing down the escalator of the Lee Gardens Hotel on their way to New Zealand. 'See you in Bangkok,' we said. It was not to be. Sting caught laryngitis in Australia, and several gigs had to be pulled. But as The Police found themselves No 1 group in Australia, they thought it wise to re-schedule the 'lost' gigs and cancel Bangkok.

Next time we were to meet was beside the pool at the Taj Mahal Hotel in Bombay. Bombay is not a city, it's an experience. Of contrast. Rich and poor. Black and white. New and old. Young and old. Past and present. Limbs and limbless. Gentility and cruelty. Life and death.

It's the most different places I've ever seen. The magnificent railway station, palm trees waving in the forecourt, looking like a palace. The jam-packed buses, the old cars. The feeling that the British were here, giving India its own imprint of magnificent architecture, awful bureaucracy. But what wonderful passivity. The beggars I was dreading . . . but they're mostly happy children, beautiful children dashing in and out of the chaotic traffic, tapping on your window, miming hunger then laughing and running away. It's total street life. Immediately one is humbled by their philosophy of life. Life? It's cheap. You just must change gear to cope, even to try to understand such a system.

We went filming in a market area, Sting and I on radio mikes. Immediately we were surrounded by a following crowd. They closed in on us enthusiastically. It was of course very hot. Every now and then a car would try to get past us, using the horn rather than the accelerator to make progress. The horde would part, slowly to let it

through. Suddenly Sting grabbed and pushed me violently out of the path of . . . a fast-moving horse, which apparently was held in as much reverence as the sacred cow, many of which were to be seen wandering through the main streets, among the double-decker buses.

Miles Copeland, the band's manager, also Stewart's elder brother, had preceded us all in Bombay, because there was a lot of setting up to do. 'You're not going to believe this,' he said, 'but the promoters are 48 middle-aged ladies.' It was true. He had charmed his way into the hearts of the Time and Talents Club, a group of ladies who put on cultural events to raise money for charity–as The Police gig was to be. They'd 'promoted' Yehudi Menuhin, the Los Angeles Symphony Orchestra, Daniel Barenboim . . . but never a Rock band. Imagine the Lady Rotarians promoting The Clash, and you'd have some idea. A whole committee was designated to help set up the show. Each member was the proud owner of a front row seat. We tried to warn them that they might find this uncomfortably LOUD, but there was no dampening their enthusiasm as first time rock fans.

When The Police arrived we went walkabout for the benefit of the film and Press cameras–in a square near the Gate of India was a man squatting on the ground, a basket in front of him, playing a pipe. Aha, we thought, he's going to charm a snake for us–well, for money. He started to play, and nothing happened. Perhaps the snake was asleep. He took the lid off and held up a cobra and shook it. He played some more. The snake collapsed into a coil and went back to sleep. True Monty Python parrot sketch stuff. Much loss of face for snake charmer. To cheer us up he staged a fight to the death between a mongoose and another snake. I was on the mongoose's side dreading the moment the snake would wrap itself around the furry animal and crush it to death. The mongoose had other ideas. With small but fierce teeth it took the initiative and began biting the snake's head with incredible speed. Within minutes the snake was a headless bloody mess. We hadn't asked for this to happen. But in India, what's another dead snake?

As we walked about the streets, teenage

boys would approach, amputated at mid-forearm. I did not discover whether this had been done deliberately by their parents at birth to make them more successful beggars. Then, the contrast. A sumptuous house on the other side of town, for lunch with one of the Time and Talents Committee. She had 16 servants, only some of whom served us an exquisite Parsee meal. Her husband was a millionaire clothes manufacturer, who supplies suits for *Take Six* and other London shops.

Of all the concerts in all the countries they had been to, Bombay was going to be the biggest test for The Police. No one in the audience would have ever seen a Rock group before, and there would be no one to sing along to their hits.

The venue was an open-air auditorium, rather curiously surrounded with buildings. It was like being in a huge concrete box open to the sky. The 'lighting' was minimal, to put it politely – a small cluster of lamps on two poles. As would befit a normal cultural event, one of the chief organizers from the Time and Talents Club stood up on the stage before the band came on to make a short speech. She was drowned out. 'I knew then it was going to be a good gig,' said Sting afterwards. He had been genuinely apprehensive that the City fathers and middle-aged husbands of the promoters, who had so generously paid a hundred rupees each for front seats, would block the kids from being able to come forward and dance. But, in the event, he need not have worried. Just one shouted encouragement and the virgin Rock 'n Roll fans had run, jumped, climbed over seats and packed themselves into a solid mass around the stage. It must have been a major triumph for Miles Copeland who, as he said, had come to India and created a demand, and a success, out of nothing.

Next day the entourage split into two. Half caught an early flight to Cairo, where wives and children were waiting. The rest of us were to have another day in India. Mike 'Biggles' Appleton, producer of the *Old Grey Whistle Test*, organized a foray in the country. We were to drive to the mountains to look at a Kali temple carved out of rock. It took an hour to drive out of the sprawling suburbs and shanty towns surrounding Bombay. Out on the dusty open road, heading towards Poona, we'd pass the occasional village and stop for a drink. Such sophistications as refrigeration do not exist in these areas. Bottled drinks were kept in tanks of murky water. But in that heat one's attitude towards hygiene becomes very abandoned! We'd just wipe the neck on a T-shirt, swig back a tepid 'Thumbs Up' – India's version of Coca Cola – and hope for the best.

Soon mountains began to loom up, and on the hair-raising hairpin bends, despite being so far from the city, again there were traffic jams! Drivers of lorries – their cabs all decorated with sequinned festoons and lurid paintings – would try for suicidal overtaking, till both sides of the road were completely blocked. After much horn sounding the drivers would jump out and discuss the snarl-up.

It was dusk before our driver found the right mountain containing the right temple. To reach the temple meant a steep climb up 350 wide steps. We had negotiated at the foot of the mountain with a guide, who showed us the carved pillars and the meditation chambers by the light of a kerosene lamp. To reach the upper chambers meant climbing out on the sheer mountainside on roughly hewn steps. I just never looked down! Night had fallen now, but the mountain was lit by brilliant moonlight.

The stillness after chaotic Bombay was exquisite. The only sounds came from a village thousands of feet below. Singing, drums banging. It was magical. Or would have been without the enthusiastic attempts of our guide, Rangoonet Toupi, to teach Stewart and me to speak Hindi. And when he wasn't talking, our attempts to enjoy the serenity and romanticism of this wonderful place were shattered by Rangoonet's gobbing, which would have impressed the most fervent early Pistols' fans.

All aspects of filming in India and later in Egypt were fraught. Indian officials were apprehensive at allowing valuable camera equipment into the country. In case we intended to sell it. Even foreign cars carry a 200 per cent import duty. Bureaucracy dictates that every customs transaction must be accompanied by countless countersigned

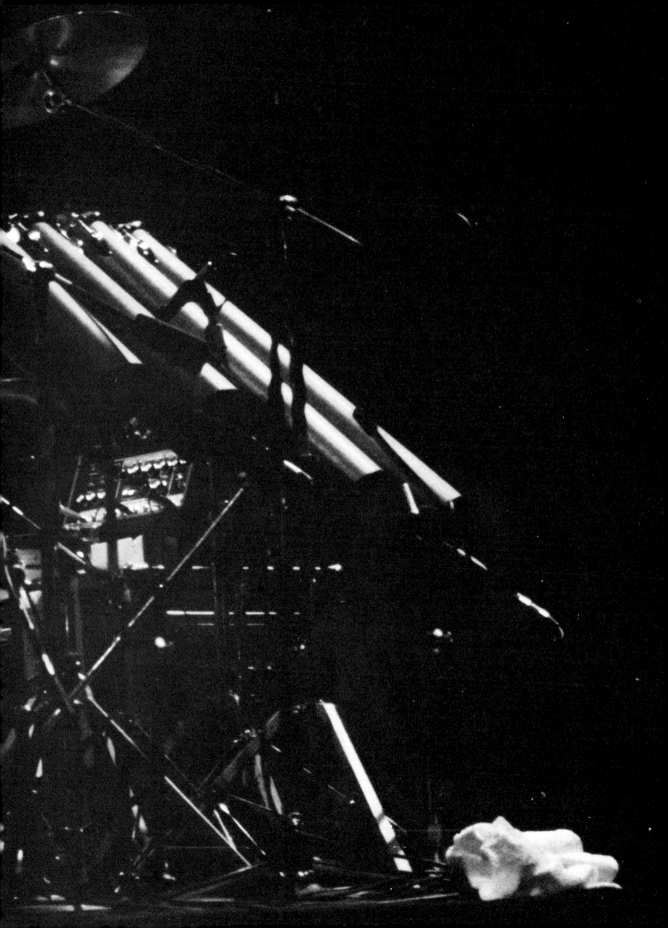

'chits', each one taking several hours to process.

The Gulf Air flight to Cairo was to stop at Dubai and Qatar. At Dubai we were informed we would have to leave our first class seats and move back to economy class at Qatar. We objected. The stewardesses were British and very sympathetic. They advised us to stay put and not move out of our seats. At Qatar various gentlemen told us we must move. We refused. It occurred to me that the airline had double booked us with a sheikh's entourage and that it was dangerous to argue with these guys—on their own airline. Impasse. The plane stayed on the ground, and we were told that if we didn't move, the flight would be delayed. We said, OK, delay the flight.

More gentlemen appeared in more menacing-looking arab dress. The documentary-conscious Stewart got out his movie camera, and zoomed in on them. That did it. One lunged at him, grabbed his camera and shouted that this was not allowed and that Stewart's film would be confiscated. Clearly the Arabs were very angry. I understand that many Arabs have a basic fear of being photographed as it is supposed to take away one's soul. In many ways I sympathise, knowing the work of some photographers!

From our next base in Cairo, surely the most exotically named of all the hotel chain, The Pyramids Holiday Inn, The Police dressed up as Arabs and we set off like some real caravan across the desert with camels, horses and carts for more filming behind the pyramids. Always there were little boys with outstretched hands saying 'Baksheesh.' Ian Copeland, the band's agent, Stewart and Miles's other brother, had arrived. He is, as is their father (an ex-CIA man) a Middle East expert and told us all we *must* haggle over all prices, otherwise we would not be respected. I was concentrating on interviewing Stewart just then, but filming him against exotic backgrounds was more difficult than we imagined. At the old citadel we were told, 'No filming. Must pay.' Back to the Sphinx. There was a glorious pink sunset over the

Pyramids. We set up again. Two gentlemen in djellabas intervened. 'Not allowed filming here. Must pay.'

The director, Derek Burbidge exploded. 'I PAID THIS MORNING. I saw the PROPER officials. I have PERMISSION.'

To no avail. 'No photograph here,' they repeated.

No one had any idea who they were. 'Let's just ignore them and carry on,' I suggested. 'They can't physically stop us.'

Derek had another idea. He positioned Stewart and me—already wired up with radio mikes—five feet away from each other, and turned the camera over and left it lying, still running, on a rock and walked away. The men in djellabas looked on. To all intents and purposes Stewart and I were just another couple of tourists admiring the Pyramids. So I had to appear very casual in asking 'Now Stewart, was the basis of The Police a direct result of the break up of Curved Air?'

Getting out of Cairo was a nightmare. There were by now 22 of us in the party, including an Australian nanny and three children. The security checks at the airport were formidable. Understandable in a country like Egypt, I suppose. The exiled Shah of Iran had arrived a week earlier and there were enough Arab factions who would hijack a plane out of Cairo, as a means of getting at Sadat, to keep the security men worried. We had to check through all hundred-odd pieces of luggage individually. Four times it was searched. We arrived, much relieved, in Athens. At last, water you could drink! No more brushing your teeth with mineral water or lemonade.

From Athens, where they had last seen a Rock gig when The Rolling Stones played there in '66, The Police followed a fairly conventional route through Europe. The final gig of the tour was a sentimental one. Yesterday The World, today—Newcastle! The City Hall was crammed with 3,000 for each of two shows. Sting's wife, the actress Frances Tomelty, commented: 'Last time he played here there were eight people in the audience—and his mum and I were two of them!' Well done, The Police.

Three gentlemen from the World Tour - Sting, Andy and (far left) Derek Burbidge, film director. Below: At the end of the day . . .

CHASE THE FADE

In case you were wondering . . .
well so was I. What to call it?
I've run radio competitions, and
picked brains – a nasty practice.
One day while driving about my
business listening to Peter
Powell on the radio, I heard him
say 'Here's Roxy Music to take
us up to the news.' But there
was just two and a half minutes
to news time. This, I realized,
would entail him 'chasing the
fade'. Fading the record out
before its natural ending. For
the last few years I've been
writing down what's been
happening before the memory
faded away . . . so that's why.

PICTURE ACKNOWLEDGMENTS

On pages with more
than one picture, the
credits read from left to
right, top to bottom.

11 Dick Barnatt
13 Colin Cavers
15 Popperfoto, C C
Weston
17 Evening Standard,
Anne Nightingale
18 C C Weston
20 Evening Standard,
Popperfoto
21 London Features
25 London Features
26–27 Rex Features

28 André Csillag
29 London Features
37 BBC Copyright
40 Colin Cavers
45 BBC Copyright
46 André Csillag
49 London Features
50 Rex Features
51 EMI Records
52 London Features
53 London Features
55 London Features
56/57 Colin Cavers
59 Trinifold Ltd
60 Christ Morphet,
Trinifold Ltd
61 London Features,
Rex Features,
Trinifold Ltd

62 Trinifold Ltd, John
Davidson
63 Syndication
International, Robert
Ellis
64 Rex Features
65 Popperfoto
67 Trinifold Ltd
69 Robert Ellis
71 Syndicational
International
73 BBC Copyright
75 André Csillag
77 André Csillag
78–79 Syndicational
International
80 Rex Features
84 Polydor
85 London Features

87 London Features
88 Stiff Records,
Polydor
89 Chrysalis, London
Features, Virgin Records
90–91 Stiff Records
93 Colin Cavers
95 Stiff Records
96–97 Colin Cavers
99 Anne Nightingale
102 A & M Records
104 A & M Records
106–107 Anne
Nightingale
112 Anne Nightingale
113 Scope Features
116–117 André Csillag
118–119 Anne
Nightingale